PIZZA

PIZZA

BY

Vincenzo Buonassisi

LITTLE, BROWN · BOSTON · TORONTO

Published simultaneously in Canada
by Little, Brown & Company (Canada) Limited

Contents

Introduction

Thousands of years ago our ancestors discovered how to cultivate grains, especially wheat. Man, long a seed gatherer, learned to store the seeds in dry pits so that he could later feed himself with pounded grain. He eventually discovered that by adding a little water to the very finely pounded grain, he could make a dough, which could be rolled out flat and roasted on hot stones. And thus bread was born.

Not much grain grew, and what did was sparse, the seeds quickly carried by the wind and scattered over the earth. The first people who collected these grains learned to recognize the most heavy bearing plants. When they tried to store them, they discovered that dampness made them rot quickly, while if they were kept dry they could be saved for leaner times. One day someone noticed that the grain thrown away in the areas around the caves and huts produced sprouts. This, like much in their lives, seemed like magic, and rituals and superstitions grew up around it. People began to select plants and sow their seeds.

The first grains were eaten whole. To make this food easier to eat, people learned to pound the grain and eventually to crush it between two rotating stones. This was the first rudimentary grindstone, the ancestor of the mill. The next step was to mix the grain with water so that it could be boiled over a fire in a stone pot. One day this primordial mush was forgotten and left on the fire until only a slightly burned pulp remained, and when someone tasted it, he discovered that it was more than edible. If that was

good, he probably reasoned, why not cook that flour-and-water mixture, formed in a flat shape, directly over the stones?

Gradually man discovered variations of those first flat breads roasted on stone, and more convenient methods for cooking. The next stage was the discovery of the principles of fermentation and the invention of the first oven. As far as we know, this came about around six thousand years ago in Egypt. There it was noted that what we call bread dough was sometimes affected by a mysterious force that made it swell up and then spoil. While most probably threw this dough away, thinking that it was impure, some must have been intrigued by it. As with most things at this time, the reaction to the affected bread varied with religious beliefs. The Hebrews, of course, long refused the "leavened" bread. The Egyptians, on the other hand, accepted this phenomenon (caused by the movement of spores in the spring air) and learned to cook the dough successfully by keeping a small piece of raw dough as a starter for the new dough. The methods for cooking this flour-and-water dough were not too different from earlier ones, though the flour surely had become finer and big clay disks were used to cook on, rather than stones.

Then the Egyptians invented an oven in the shape of a cone, of which we have evidence today. The cook lit a fire inside the cone and then literally stuck the bread onto the outside. When it fell it was done on one side and was then re-stuck to finish cooking the other.

It was only later that they thought of dividing the inside of the oven in two and making a fire in one half and putting the leavened dough in the other to cook.

By that time there were certainly many varieties of bread. Bread itself had taken on a mythological importance in most cultures, and was used as an offering to the divinities. It was seasoned in appetizing ways for all sorts of religious festivities, a practice that has continued down through the centuries to our own era.

Some breads were enriched with olives and pork scraps, the forerunners of what today are known in Italy as *focaccia* and *torta rustica*. Honey, raisins, and pine nuts were added to others, and they eventually became the various *panettone*, *pangiallo*, *pan dolce* and so on. The Greeks and Romans had similar foods, and thanks to the poet Virgil, we have the recipe for *moretum*, which was nothing more than a flat circle of unleavened dough, baked in the oven, then moistened with oil and vinegar and eaten with raw onion, or possibly with garlic. This was a forerunner of the Italian *schiacciata*, and, if you take it one step farther and let the dough rise, you have the beginnings of pizza.

The first primitive *schiacciata*, which was an accompaniment to Italian life from Roman times through the medieval period and beyond, is again referred to during the period around the year 1000 A.D. In that period in Naples, the bread was called *lagano*, instead of *schiacciata*, a word which comes from the Latin *laganum* and the Greek *laganon*. This was a *schiacciata* of unleavened dough, roasted and cut into strips that were then tossed into a pot of vegetables or other ingredients cooking over the fire. In short, it was a kind of primitive *tagliatelle*, and, in fact, on the islands of Sicily and Sardinia *tagliatelle* is still called *laganella* and the rolling pin is called a *laganaturo*. Horace, the Roman poet, speaks gluttonously of a soup of chick-peas, leeks, and *lagano*, from southern Italy. (The dish is still made there, only now the strips of dough are fried for the sake of simplicity.) While they still spoke of *lagano* in Naples around the year 1000, the word *picea* also began to appear. This might have either been another name for *lagano* or indicated a new dish: a circle of dough covered with colorful and flavorful ingredients before baking. Shortly after, the word *piza* began appearing. (Even today, in southern Italy, the word pizza refers not only to a seasoned *schiacciata*, put in the oven and baked, but also to circles of dough that have been stuffed and fried.)

We must wait until the eighteenth century to reach the pizza most people know today, the version made with tomatoes. The reason for its tardy appearance is that tomatoes did not exist in Europe until they were introduced there from America. It took a century and a half for Europeans to discover the possibilities for using tomatoes in cooking and for the Neapolitans, in particular, to make it part of their cuisine. Pizza with a tomato sauce, then, is a comparatively recent arrival. It was this pizza, however, that gained worldwide popularity and has come to represent pizza itself, in pizzerias all over the world.

But let's not lose the thread of our story. Toward the end of the eighteenth century, in Naples, the pizza began to emerge on its own. The first ones were probably those made with oil and garlic, with Mozzarella and salted anchovies, or covered with the tiny fish called *cicinielli*. They also spoke of a pizza filled and folded over, which was probably an early form of *calzone*. And, of course, the tomato pizza.

Until about 1830, pizza was sold from open-air stands. But then a true pizzeria, called Port'Alba, appeared in Naples. It had a brick-lined oven fired by wood. That was soon replaced with an oven lined with Vesuvian lapillus (lava), which was better able to reach the high temperatures needed to make the best pizzas. This pizzeria later became the haunt of artists and writers, and perhaps it was there that D'Annunzio wrote the lines for one of his most beautiful

Neapolitan songs, *A vucchella*. Almost certainly among the celebrated guests was Salvatore di Giacomo, who dedicated several poems to pizza.

From its first appearance in the nineteenth century, pizza has inspired many poets, writers and musicians. Alexandre Dumas, the author of *The Three Musketeers*, put together sharp observations and odd information about pizza, in a series of travel essays that were collected in the *Corricolo*. For example, he wrote that "the pizza is a kind of stiacciata (*sic*) which is made in St. Denis: it is round in shape and made with bread dough. At first glance it looks like a simple food, but examined more closely, it seems complicated." He was right, and the reference to the *schiacciata* of St. Denis confirms that the pizza form is universal, while the garnishing and cooking of the most famous version are completely Neapolitan.

Dumas also notes the various kinds of pizza, the most common ones at the beginning of the nineteenth century being those with oil, lard, pork fat, cheese, tomatoes, and little fish (like *cicinielli*). And he casually mentions a pizza called "a otto," which he says was baked a week before it was eaten. Here, however, he made a gross error. The pizza "for eight" was actually eaten right away but was paid for eight days later, even though these easy terms increased its cost a little. This custom lasted for years and perhaps still exists even today.

Finally pizza is often mentioned in a famous work, *Usi e costumi di Napoli* (The Customs of Naples), by a completely Neapolitanized author with a French name, De Bourcard. I quote from the text, written around 1850: "Pizza is not found in the 'vocabolario della Crusca' [the Florentine group which worked to maintain the purity of the Italian language], because it is made with flour [still considered vulgar at that time] and because it is a specialty of Neapolitans, in fact, of the very city of Naples. Take a piece of dough, pull or spread it with a rolling pin or push it out with the palm of the hand, put whatever comes into your head on it, season it with oil or lard, bake it in the oven, eat it and you will know what a pizza is. Though more or less the same, the *focaccia* and the *schiacciata* are but embryos of the art." In the same text he lists the kinds of pizza most in use. There were oil and garlic pizzas, pizzas with grated cheese, lard, basil, or tiny fish, or those with Mozzarella, ham or mussels, or tomato, though this last one he did not consider of great importance.

Thus we come to the end of the nineteenth century and a famous episode. The year was 1889. That summer King Umberto I went with Queen Margherita to Naples to the Capodimonte palace, because as monarch he was required to visit the kingdom of the islands of Sicily and Sardinia. The queen was curious about pizza. She had never eaten it but she had heard much about it from writers and artists who visited the court. Since she could not go to a pizzeria, the pizzeria had to come to her. The most famous pizzamaker of the time, Don Raffaele Esposito, owner of the celebrated pizzeria Pietro il Pizzaiuolo, was called to court.

Don Raffaele came, he saw, and he conquered. Using the ovens in the royal kitchen, and assisted by his wife, Donna Rosa, who was the true mistress of pizza, he prepared one with pork fat, cheese, and basil, one with garlic, oil, and tomatoes, and another with Mozzarella, tomatoes, and fresh basil, which were the colors of the Italian flag. This last one particularly pleased Queen Margherita, and not just for patriotic motives. Don Raffaele, a good public relations man, had named the pizza "alla Margherita," and the next day added it to his menu. As you can imagine, it caught on. As the story spread beyond Naples, so did the popularity of the dish, and it was simply called "pizza Margherita." (In fact, what passed as a genuine creation had already existed. It was not considered among the most classic and important pizzas, but it was already being made in Naples. The Bourbon queen, Maria Carolina, who was such a glutton for pizza that she wanted an oven built in her palace, also loved that red, white, and green pizza. Alas, those colors did not bode well for her dynasty.)

Certainly the Margherita helped to spread the Neapolitan pizza, first to northern Italy and then to the world. The two pizzas which have traveled the farthest are the Margherita and the Neapolitan, which is made like the Margherita but with anchovies added. However, as we have seen, others preceded them and boasted of authentic Neapolitan origins as well. By now there are many more kinds of pizza and they are all delicious.

PIZZA

Sesame-Soy Beef Stir-Fry

1 pound beef round tip steaks, cut 1/8 to 1/4 inch thick
1 package (16 ounces) frozen stir-fry vegetable mixture
2 teaspoons cornstarch dissolved in 1/3 cup water
Hot cooked rice (optional)
1/4 cup chopped toasted walnuts (optional)

Marinade:

3 tablespoons soy sauce
2 teaspoons dark sesame oil

1. Combine marinade ingredients in medium bowl. Remove and reserve 2 tablespoons. Stack beef steaks; cut lengthwise in half, then crosswise into 1-inch wide strips. Add beef to remaining marinade; toss.
2. Heat large nonstick skillet over medium-high heat until hot. Add 1/2 of beef; stir-fry 1 minute or until outside surface of beef is no longer pink. (Do not overcook.) Remove. Repeat with remaining beef.
3. Combine vegetables and 1/4 cup water in same skillet; cook over medium-high heat 4 to 5 minutes or until most of water is evaporated and vegetables are hot, stirring occasionally. Combine cornstarch mixture and reserved marinade. Add to vegetables; cook and stir 1 minute or until thickened and bubbly. Add beef; heat through. Serve over rice. Sprinkle with walnuts.

Makes 4 servings.   Total preparation and cooking time: 25 minutes

65391 3/04 PRINTING & SUPPLY

How to Make Pizza

How do you make pizza? First of all, let's start with the dough. The classic recipe we know is the one used for bread dough — flour, yeast, salt, and water. In Italy, you can buy bread dough from a bakery as well as make it at home. In either case, the dough requires particular attention and care to get the best pizza. Let's look at how it is done.

We will start with enough dough to make six individual pizzas — small to medium depending on how thinly you roll them out. You will need:

2 cubes (⅔ ounce) compressed yeast or 2 envelopes (¼ ounce) dry yeast

½ cup lukewarm water

7 cups bread flour, approximately (all-purpose flour can be used, but bread flour is best)

1 teaspoon salt

Olive oil (optional)

Stir the yeast into the warm water and let it sit for 10 minutes. Add one cup of flour to form a very soft starter dough. Cover with a cloth and let rest in a warm place for about an hour. Add 1¾ cups water (olive oil can be substituted for ¼ cup of the water for a slightly softer crust) and the salt, mixing well. Start adding the flour, a cup at a time, until the dough becomes too stiff to stir. Turn it out on a floured board and continue kneading in the rest of the flour, using the heel of your hand to push

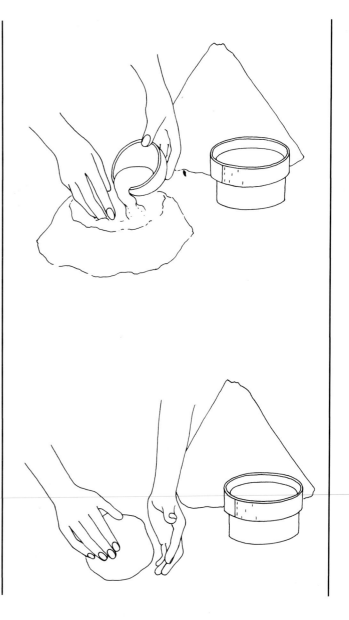

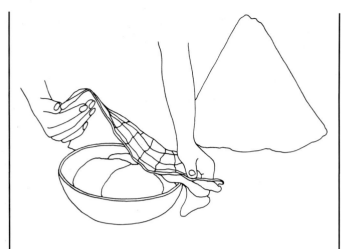

At this point, divide the dough into six portions, place them on a floured surface and cover with a cloth to rise again. They should double in size. You should judge this by eye; usually it will take 1 to 2 hours.

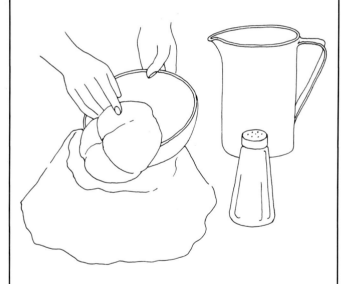

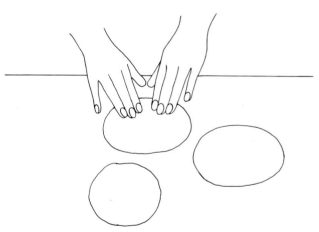

forward and pull back. This kneading will take about 10 minutes or more and is done to eliminate the excess gas produced by the risen dough, which could interfere with the baking process. As you work, the dough should become smoother and more elastic.

Now punch them down again and knead until each can be worked into a circle. Accomplished pizzamakers enjoy doing acrobatics with the dough, throwing the circle of dough in the air and catching it without its losing shape or folding, to show just how elastic the dough is.

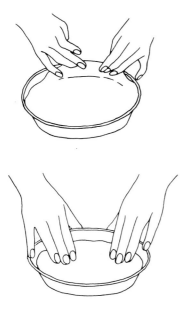

How big and how thick should the circle be? In general the dough should be thin, but from there there are two schools of thought, the classic Neapolitan and the Roman. Neapolitan pizza should be approximately ⅛ inch thick, with the center a little thinner and the edges a little thicker. The edges will puff up during baking, forming a rim that serves to keep the ingredients in the center. The Roman school of thought says that the dough should be thinner, approximately 1/16 inch, and needs no rim as the toppings are less fluid and so tend to stay in place. In reality it is not so much a question of schools as of what you put on top. Remember that pizza was originally a very simple dish.

Now the dough is ready to be filled with the ingredients from one of the recipes and placed in the oven. *The oven should be preheated to 400°F;* baking should be short and intense. Ideally it is baked in a brick oven or one lined with volcanic rock and fueled with wood, but since few of us have such ovens, a gas or electric stove will do just fine. Ceramic baking tiles, which simulate the effect of a brick oven, are commercially available.

In traditional pizzamaking the pizza is placed in the oven with a long-handled flat wooden spatula and it is handled as adroitly as the dough. The pizzamaker watches the progress of the pizza through the oven window and knows exactly when to remove it so that it slides perfectly cooked onto the serving plate. But when is the exact moment? If the pizza has a rim, it is easy to tell — it is when the dough becomes gold brown and small blisters develop on its surface. These blisters are caused by small bubbles of air, formed by the heat, bursting. If the pizza has no rim, one must look at the edges; they should also be baked to a golden brown. It is not as easy to check in ovens without windows, but when the Mozzarella or other cheeses look melted or when the other ingredients take on a shiny appearance because of the oil they were moistened with, the pizza is ready, usually in about 10 to 15 minutes.

And the shape? Up to now we have discussed only the traditional round shape, but there is also pizza-by-the-inch, which became famous a few decades ago in the Sorrento peninsula. It is baked on a rectangular pan with or without a rim and is then cut by the inch or the foot as you wish.

And finally, how do you eat pizza? Let's be very clear about this. You should always eat pizza with your hands, just as they do in Naples. It doesn't make sense to subject a pizza to the torture of knife and fork while it cools, losing its flavor and aroma. Of course the original pizza, not very large and not heavily sauced, was easy to fold in half and eat, if one took care not to drip the oil, Mozzarella, and tomato. However, today's pizzas are bigger and richer, and therein lies the problem. The simplest solution is to cut the pizza into four or six pieces, fold it, and eat the big slices with your hands. This works very well and the delightful flavor and aroma are not lost.

There are many pizza recipes in this book, but I wanted to include all the traditional ones along with their many variations. I also wanted to add others that might be called fantasy versions or personal creations, and those from other pizzamakers inspired by the regions they came from and the places where they work. I could have added many more of this sort of recipe but I finally had to choose only those which had some special character and leave out others which I hope you'll discover someday.

I have also added many recipes that are connected to pizza in other parts of Italy and the world: the *schiacciate*, and the *focaccia*, which have common roots, as I discussed earlier. Taking that as a starting point, I have extended the collection to include those savory rustic pies made with the original flour-and-water dough and then enriched with oil or lard or even eggs and other ingredients. This includes all the pizza, *pizzelle*, *sgonfiotti*, and *schiacciate* that are fried instead of baked. I hope that they give you a wider repertoire for your table, because all the recipes have been given so that they can be easily made at home.

The dough recipe is not repeated in each recipe but instead is given once at the beginning of this section. The quantities given are enough for six medium pizzas. You can add or subtract proportionally to make more or fewer pizzas, or bigger or smaller ones. However, one word of advice: if you want to make many pizzas, it is better to make the dough in two or more batches, as it is easier to work with that way and the rising takes place more easily.

The amounts given for the ingredients for the toppings are only a general guide. You can use greater or smaller amounts without affecting the cooking. Of course it is better not to exaggerate and make the pizza so rich that the ingredients do not cook well, or so scant that the ingredients cook too fast. The basic ingredients such as Mozzarella and other cheeses and tomatoes should always be in large enough quantities to cover the complete base of the dough, leaving only a small border. They should not, however, be thicker than the thickness of the dough itself. Garnishes such as slices of sausage or bacon or anchovies should be just enough to add flavor without overwhelming the pizza. Canned tomatoes, drained well and crushed, can be substituted for fresh tomatoes. But I repeat, there are few hard and fast rules regarding pizza; with a little care you can't go wrong.

In the other recipes, I have tried to indicate the amounts and procedures required for preparation in each case. This is because there are many variations, even though minimal, and I know from experience that it can be annoying to have to constantly refer back to previous pages. The only exception to this is when a series of similar recipes are grouped together, such as the many varieties of *torta rustica*, where only the ingredients in the fillings change.

Most of the ingredients needed to prepare the recipes in this book—fresh meats, cheeses, and vegetables—are available at any grocery. Sometimes, however, a recipe will call for special Italian ingredients, but will also list, wherever possible, a readily available American substitute. Most cities and large towns have an Italian neighborhood or shop that carries most of the specialty items called for. Such shops are often a delight in themselves, and the true Italian flavor of your pizza, *crostata*, or *calzone* will be well worth the trip.

One of the pizza's many charms is that it can be made with the most basic kitchen equipment: a baking sheet or pie pan, a household oven, and a knife. There are, however, a few pieces of special equipment that you might find useful. Ceramic oven tiles, which simulate the effect of a brick pizza oven, are commercially available. Place the tiles in the oven before preheating, and place the pan directly on top of them. Round pizza bricks perform the same function, but the pizza can be placed directly on top of the brick, by using a wooden pizza paddle. When the pizza is cooked, slide the paddle underneath the pizza and remove it from the oven. Round pizza pans with a low rim are useful if you are making pizzas with lots of toppings that might be too heavy or wet for just the rim of the crust to support. Some people like to use pizza wheels to cut the finished pizza, but I find that they never work in the corners of the pan and that a large, sharp knife works just as well.

PART ONE

Pizza, schiacciata, calzone

1
PIZZA WITH OIL AND GARLIC

The custom of eating slices of bread seasoned with oil and garlic as an accompaniment to pasta dishes is surely a very old one. Oil and garlic were first used to flavor and enrich the taste of the *schiacciata*, a kind of pita bread traditionally eaten in Italy, and then with pizza.

Basic dough recipe (page 15)
¼–½ cup olive oil
6–12 cloves garlic, to taste, thinly sliced
Salt and pepper

Roll out the dough into six small circles or two large ones and bake in a preheated 400° oven until golden brown. Remove from the oven and moisten the top with olive oil, sprinkle with the garlic slices, salt and pepper, and serve hot.

2
PIZZA BAKED WITH OIL AND GARLIC

This recipe varies from the previous one in that you moisten the unbaked dough with olive oil, sprinkle sliced garlic and salt over it, and then bake. A pinch of oregano or rosemary can be added for flavor. Pepper should only be used after the pizza has baked.

3
PIZZA WITH LARD AND CHEESE, No. 1

This is another very old version of pizza. To serve six people you will need:

Basic dough recipe (page 15)
⅓ cup lard, melted
2 cups Provolone, Pecorino, or Caciocavallo cheese, grated
Fresh basil

Brush the dough lightly with the lard, sprinkle with the grated cheese, and garnish with a few

Pizza with Oil and Garlic

leaves of fresh basil. Remember that fresh basil leaves should never be washed or they lose their fragrance. Simply wipe each leaf with a soft cloth. Bake in a preheated 400° oven until golden.

4
PIZZA WITH LARD AND CHEESE, No. 2

This recipe is similar to number 1 except that after you brush the dough with the lard, you sprinkle about 3 cups of Mozzarella in cubes over it, followed by finely grated Pecorino, Provolone, or Caciocavallo cheese. On top you may garnish the pizza with a few fresh basil leaves. Then bake it in a preheated 400° oven until golden.

5
PIZZA WITH TOMATOES AND BASIL

This is one of the most basic recipes.

Basic dough recipe (page 15)
4–6 medium tomatoes, peeled and seeded
Fresh basil leaves
Salt and pepper
Olive oil

Drop the tomatoes in boiling water for a moment or two to make peeling easier, then remove seeds and watery interior (to keep dough from becoming soggy). Cut the tomatoes into wedges. Roll the dough out very thin and then cover with the tomatoes. On top spread a large handful of fresh basil, either whole or chopped. Sprinkle with salt and pepper, moisten with oil, and bake in a preheated 400° oven until the crust is brown.

6
NEAPOLITAN PIZZA

This is considered the most traditional pizza today. It is really the descendant of the original oil and garlic pizza.

Basic dough recipe (page 15)
4–6 medium tomatoes, peeled and seeded (see above) then sliced or chopped
Oregano or fresh basil
4 cloves garlic, finely sliced
Olive oil
Salt

Place the tomatoes on the circles of dough. Sprinkle some oregano over them or some basil leaves, carefully wiped clean but not washed, or both. Add the finely sliced garlic to taste, then dribble olive oil over the whole pizza, add salt, and place it in a preheated 400° oven.

Pizza with Tomatoes and Basil

7
PIZZA ALLA MARINARA

This is another variation of one of the most traditional pizzas. It is similar to the Neapolitan pizza except that it omits oregano and basil.

Basic dough recipe (page 15)
4–6 medium tomatoes, peeled, seeded and sliced (see page 23)

4 cloves garlic, finely sliced
6–12 anchovy fillets, to taste
Olive oil
Black olives (optional)

Place the tomatoes and garlic on the dough, then scatter small pieces of anchovies over the surface. Finally dribble olive oil over the entire filling and bake in a preheated 400° oven until golden.

Note: Often the anchovies are de-boned and chopped, then added as they are, to the other ingredients. However you might prefer to wash them first to remove some of the salty flavor, which can be rather overpowering.

A common variation is to add slices of black olives to the basic pizza, as their flavor goes very well with the other ingredients.

8
PIZZA MARGHERITA

As we learned in the introduction, Pizza Margherita takes its name from Queen Margherita of Savoy. It was first served to her one evening in 1889 at a party in the Capodimonte palace in Naples. The queen loved it, not only for its taste but for its red, white, and green colors as well.

You will need:

Basic pizza dough (page 15)
4–6 medium tomatoes, peeled, seeded and cut into strips (see page 23)
1 pound Mozzarella cheese, cut into thin slices
Fresh basil
Salt
Olive oil

Clean the basil leaves, wiping them with a soft cloth. Do not wash them. Roll out the dough and cover with strips of tomatoes. Cover with cheese slices. Then scatter the basil leaves over the top, salt to taste, and moisten the top with a little olive oil. Bake in a preheated 400° oven until golden.

9
PIZZA ROMAN STYLE

You will need:

Basic pizza dough (page 15)
4–6 medium tomatoes, peeled, seeded and cut into wedges (see page 23)
1 pound Mozzarella cheese, sliced
12 anchovy fillets
Fresh basil
Olive oil

Roll out the dough very thin so that when it bakes it will become crisp. Spread the tomatoes on the dough, then the Mozzarella slices, the anchovies, and a few basil

Pizza alla Marinara (left)
Pizza Margherita (right)

leaves, and dribble oil over the whole circle. Bake in a preheated 400° oven until golden and crisp.

Try oregano instead of basil, or add finely grated Romano.

Pizza with Onions, No. 1

10
PIZZA WITH ONIONS, No. 1

You will need:

Basic dough recipe (page 15)
4 medium onions, sliced thin
1¼ cups grated Pecorino or Romano cheese
Olive oil

Spread a layer of onions on the rounds of dough and on top of them, sprinkle the grated cheese, enough to cover. Then moisten the whole pizza with oil and put in a preheated 400° oven and bake until golden. It will look like a brightly shining sun on the plate. Many add a sprinkling of freshly ground pepper after it is baked.

11
PIZZA WITH ONIONS, No. 2

This recipe is identical to the one above except that you spread a tablespoon of tomato pulp on the dough first, then the onions, the cheese, and the oil. The pizza

comes out with a delicate and pleasing rosy color.

12
PIZZA WITH ONIONS, No. 3

You will need:

Basic pizza dough (page 15)
6 medium onions
Olive oil
2 medium tomatoes, peeled, seeded and crushed (see page 23)
Salt and pepper
1½ cups Mozzarella cheese, in cubes
12 anchovies (to taste)
1½ cups grated Pecorino or Romano cheese

Slice the onions and sauté in a little oil until translucent. Do not let them brown. Add the crushed tomatoes to the onion, along with salt and pepper to taste. Spread this sauce over the rolled-out dough, add the Mozzarella and the anchovies, and top with grated Pecorino or Romano. Bake in a preheated 400° oven until golden and cheese is melted.

In Sardinia, where this recipe is popular, oregano is often mixed in with the grated cheese before it is strewn over the pizza.

13
PIZZA PUGLIESE STYLE

You will need:

Basic dough recipe (page 15)
Fresh basil
2 cloves garlic, finely sliced
½ cup chopped parsley
3 cups chopped tomatoes, peeled and seeded (see page 23)
1½ cups grated Pecorino or Romano cheese
Oregano
Pepper

Wipe the basil leaves clean with soft dry cloth (do not wash), then chop with the garlic and parsley, mixing well. Roll out circles of dough, spread the chopped tomato over the circles, then spread the garlic, basil and parsley mixture. Sprinkle the grated cheese and a pinch of oregano over each one and put into a preheated 400° oven and bake until the crust is golden and the cheese has melted. When it is done and on the table, grind some black pepper over it.

14
PIZZA WITH GREENS, No. 1

You will need:

Basic pizza dough (page 15)
6 cups fresh spinach or beet greens
1½ cups grated Parmesan, Pecorino, or Provolone cheese
Olive oil

Wash the greens well, dry them, then chop them finely. Roll out the dough, making six circles; they should not be too thin. Spread the spinach or beet greens over each one and generously sprinkle the cheese over them, mashing it into the greens a little. Moisten each circle with a little oil, sprinkle with salt, and place in a preheated 400° oven until golden. Eat this while it is hot and crispy.

15
PIZZA WITH GREENS, No. 2

In this version you can mix beet greens, spinach, chicory or other greens together, chopping finely. The rest is the same as the first version.

16
PIZZA WITH PEPPERS, No. 1

You will need:

Basic pizza dough (page 15)
6 medium green peppers
3 cups tomatoes, peeled, seeded and chopped (see page 23)
Salt and pepper

Roast the peppers first, either on a long fork directly over the fire or under the broiler, turning frequently. The skin will blacken and peel easily. Then cut them into strips. Roll out thin circles of dough and spread the chopped tomatoes over them. Lay the pepper strips on top, and salt to taste.

Bake in a preheated 400° oven until the crust is golden and the peppers are soft. When it is done, sprinkle with coarsely ground pepper and eat while it is crisp and hot.

17
PIZZA WITH PEPPERS, No. 2

In this version, spread grated cheese over the peppers. You will need approximately 1½ cups. Pecorino is the preferred cheese, but Parmesan, Swiss, and Caciocavallo also work well.

Pizza with Greens, No. 2 (below)
Pizza with Green Peppers, No. 1 (right)

18
PIZZA WITH ONIONS AND PEPPERS, No. 1

Basic pizza dough (page 15)
1½ cups chopped onions
3 medium peppers, prepared as on
    page 28
Olive oil

Spread a mixture of chopped onions and green peppers over the rolled-out dough. Sprinkle with oil and bake in a preheated 400° oven until the peppers have become soft and the onion is cooked. The proportions of peppers to onions can be modified, using more onion and less pepper, or you can use both red and green peppers, giving the pizza an attractive bright color.

19
PIZZA WITH ONIONS AND PEPPERS, No. 2

This recipe is similar to the one above, but you can add slices of Mozzarella and a pinch of salt. If you have used both red and green peppers, it makes a perfect color combination.

20
PIZZA WITH ONIONS AND PEPPERS, No. 3

In this version sauté the chopped onions in a little oil until translucent but not brown. Add the peppers, roasted and peeled as on page 28, either chopped or cut into strips, and let them cook with the onion a few minutes. Drain the onions and peppers well to get rid of as much of the cooking oil as possible, then spread them over the rolled-out dough. Dribble a little fresh oil over them, salt lightly and bake in a preheated 400° oven until the dough is golden brown.

21
PIZZA WITH ONIONS AND PEPPERS, No. 4

Still another variation, this one uses celery. You will need:

Basic dough recipe (page 15)
1½ cups sliced onions
¼ cup finely chopped celery
Olive oil

3 medium green peppers, prepared as
  on page 28
Salt

Lightly brown the chopped onions and celery in a little oil; when they are both translucent, add the chopped green pepper. Stir and let them cook together a few minutes. Drain the mixture well, spread it over the rolled-out dough, and moisten the pizzas with some fresh

oil and a little salt. Bake in a preheated 400° oven and serve hot.

22
PIZZA WITH ZUCCHINI, No. 1

You will need:

Basic dough recipe (page 15)
4–6 small zucchini
Olive oil

Salt
½ cup chopped parsley
1 pound Mozzarella cheese, sliced

Wash the zucchini, cut them into slices or cubes, and sauté with a little oil, salt, and the parsley. Remove from the heat and drain well. Spread the mixture over the rolled-out dough and add the slices of Mozzarella. Dribble some fresh oil over the circles of dough, sprinkle with a little salt, and bake in a preheated 400° oven until golden. Serve hot.

23
PIZZA WITH ZUCCHINI, No. 2

This is the same recipe as described above, with the variation of adding tomatoes, giving it a reddish color. When you sauté the zucchini, add a tablespoon or two of tomato pulp or, better yet, peeled and seeded tomatoes cut in chunks (see page 23). Let the zucchini and tomato cook a few minutes, then pour the mixture over the pizza dough as in the preceding recipe, moisten with a little fresh oil, and bake in a preheated 400° oven until golden.

In this second version you can also add pitted and chopped green or black olives, to taste. This pizza is also best served immediately.

*Pizza with Onions and Peppers, No. 3
(left)*
Pizza with Zucchini, No. 1 (right)

Pizza with Cardoons

24
PIZZA WITH SQUASH BLOSSOMS

If you grow zucchini or other squash in the garden, the squash blossoms make a very delicate pizza. You will need:

Basic dough recipe (page 15)
¾ cup chopped onions
Olive oil
¾ cup squash blossoms, cut into small strips
Salt and pepper

Sauté the chopped onions in a little oil until translucent, then add the squash blossoms, salt, and pepper. Cook them very briefly and cover the pizza with this sauce. Put in a preheated 400° oven and cook until the crust is golden.

You can also scatter raw onion over the dough and then sprinkle with zucchini blossoms that have been cut in strips and very briefly sautéed in oil. Sprinkle with salt and pepper and bake.

25
PIZZA WITH FENNEL

You will need:
Basic dough recipe (page 15)

1 small onion, finely chopped
Olive oil
3 medium stalks of fennel, thinly sliced
Salt and pepper
1½ cups grated Parmesan or Pecorino cheese

Make a *soffritto* by gently sautéing the onions in a little oil, then add the sliced fennel and let it brown a little so that it loses its raw quality. Drain well, add salt and pepper, and then spread this mixture over the rolled-out dough. Sprinkle each round with grated cheese, moisten with a little oil,

Pizza with Asparagus Tips

and bake in a preheated 400° oven until golden.

26
PIZZA WITH CARDOONS

These are a kind of white thistle found in Italy, called *cardi*. Cooked burdock stems can be substituted. You will need about 3 cups. Slice them and sauté briefly in olive oil, then drain well and follow the recipe for Pizza with Fennel, above.

27
PIZZA WITH ASPARAGUS TIPS

Basic dough recipe (page 15)
36 thin stalks of asparagus
4 anchovy fillets
Olive oil
1½ cups grated Parmesan or
    Pecorino cheese

Parboil the asparagus stalks for 5 minutes, then drain well. Mash the anchovies and mix with the oil, making a little sauce. Spread this over the rolled-out dough. Trim the asparagus stalks and arrange them over the dough. Cover the asparagus with grated cheese. Bake in a preheated 400° oven until the cheese melts and the asparagus is cooked.

You can also add a little tomato pulp or peeled and seeded tomatoes (see page 23) cut in wedges or chopped.

28
PIZZA WITH BROCCOLI OR TURNIP GREENS

You will need:

Basic dough recipe (page 15)
3 cups chopped broccoli or turnip
    greens
1 small green pepper, chopped
2 cloves garlic, sliced thin
2 anchovy fillets
Olive oil

Clean and parboil the broccoli or turnip greens, and cut into pieces. Set aside but keep them warm. In a frying pan, sauté the green pepper,

garlic, and anchovies in a little oil. Mix this with the broccoli or turnip greens, spread over the rolled-out dough, and bake in a preheated 400° oven until the crust is golden and the broccoli is tender.

29
PIZZA WITH OLIVES

Olives are present in many kinds of pizza as a side ingredient, but in this pizza they play the main role. You will need:

Basic dough recipe (page 15)
3 cups chopped tomatoes, peeled and

seeded (see page 23)
2 cups Mozzarella cheese, cubed
1½ cups green olives, pitted and
   chopped
Olive oil

Spread the tomatoes over the rolled-out dough, add the Mozzarella and the green olives, dribble oil over each circle, and bake in a preheated 400° oven until the cheese has melted and the crust is browned.

In other versions you can add a few pieces of anchovy, about 1 fillet per small pizza, and some capers. You can also eliminate the tomato. Black olives can also be used instead of green, but they have a stronger flavor, so fewer should be used.

30
PIZZA WITH OLIVE CAVIAR

The pizza is given this name mostly in jest. Olive caviar consists of olives that have been left to marinate in herbs and oil, usually marjoram, thyme or whatever is on hand. It comes from Liguria, but can be found in gourmet stores carrying Italian products. You will need:

Basic dough recipe (page 15)
½ cup olive caviar
3 cups Mozzarella cheese, cubed
Olive oil

Mix the olive caviar, which is strongly flavored, with cubes of cheese Cover the rolled-out dough with this mixture and moisten with

a little oil. Bake in a preheated 400° oven until the crust is golden and the cheese melted.

For variation, first spread some tomato pulp over the dough, then the olive and cheese mixture, and proceed as above.

31
PIZZA WITH SHALLOTS, No. 1

Shallots are a kind of wild onion called *lampascioni* in Puglia and other regions in the south where they grow wild, deep in the ground. They have a slightly bitter taste that many people like, but this can be reduced by cutting off the dark end of the shallot. You will need:

Basic dough recipe (page 15)
12 shallots
1½ cups grated Pecorino or Romano
   cheese
Olive oil
Salt and pepper

Clean the shallots, peel, and slice finely. Roll out thin circles of dough and scatter the shallots over each one. Sprinkle the cheese over this, moisten with a little oil, and season with salt. Bake in a preheated 400° oven. When it is golden brown, remove from the oven and sprinkle coarsely ground pepper over it.

32
PIZZA WITH SHALLOTS, No. 2

In this version, clean and peel the shallots, then boil them in a

large pan of salted water until tender. Drain well and mash them a little. Moisten the shallots with olive oil, sprinkle with salt and pepper, and let them cool. Then spread them over the dough and bake as in the first version.

33
PIZZA WITH EGGPLANT, No. 1

You will need:

Basic dough recipe (page 15)
1 large eggplant
Salt
Olive oil
3 cups tomato pulp
2 cups Mozzarella cheese
Oregano
Pepper

First prepare the eggplant. Cut off the stalk end and cut the eggplant in small cubes, removing the inside pulp with the seeds, but leaving the skin on. Put the cubes in a colander, salt well, and let them sit for an hour or more so that the bitter liquid drains off. Then dry them well and fry in a generous amount of oil. Drain the cubes. Meanwhile prepare the tomato pulp by peeling and seeding the tomatoes as on page 23, then crush them and force through a sieve. On each circle spread a generous amount of the tomato pulp, then on top scatter the eggplant, thin slices of Mozzarella, and a pinch of oregano and pepper. Moisten it with oil and bake in a preheated 400° oven until the crust is brown.

Pizza with Shallots, No. 1

34
PIZZA WITH EGGPLANT, No. 2

This recipe is similar to the preceding one. Instead of sautéing the eggplant in a lot of oil, use only a small amount and add tomato pulp, garlic slices, and finally a pinch of oregano and chopped olives. When the ingredients are cooked, spread the mixture over the dough, cover with the Mozzarella, moisten with a little fresh oil, and bake as in the first version.

35
PIZZA WITH CURLY ENDIVE, No. 1

You will need:

Basic dough recipe (page 15)
One head curly endive
Olive oil
3 anchovy fillets
2 tablespoons capers
3 tablespoons chopped black or green
    olives

Clean and parboil the endive and cut it into strips. Heat a few tablespoons of oil in a skillet and brown the endive with a few small pieces of anchovy, the capers, and the olives. Stir it a few times and let it cook over low heat for about 10 minutes. Pour the mixture over the dough (which should be somewhat thicker than usual) and bake in a preheated 400° oven until the dough is golden.

Pizza with Eggplant, No. 2

36
PIZZA WITH CURLY ENDIVE, No. 2

In this version, raisins and pine nuts are added in place of the anchovies, capers, and olives. You will need ¼ cup of raisins (revive them first by soaking in warm water — allow to drain thoroughly) and ¼ cup of pine nuts. Add the pine nuts and raisins to the browned endive, and proceed the same as in the preceding recipe. The raisins and pine nuts can also be added after the endive mixture is spread over the dough. This recipe was suggested to me by Franco Simione, a pizzamaker of the Bruschetta restaurant in Milan.

37
PIZZA WITH ARTICHOKES, No. 1

You will need:

Basic dough recipe (page 15)
3 medium to large artichokes (or use canned artichoke hearts, well-drained)
Lemon juice in water
1½ cups Mozzarella cheese, thinly sliced
Salt and pepper

Clean the artichokes and remove the hearts. Cut the hearts into thin slices, and if you have to set them aside, put them in the lemon juice and water so that they don't discolor. When you are ready to make the pizza, spread the well-drained artichoke hearts over the dough, add thin slices of Mozzarella, season with salt and pepper, and bake in a preheated 400° oven until the crust is golden and the cheese has melted.

You can substitute any other soft cheese for the Mozzarella.

38
PIZZA WITH ARTICHOKES, No. 2

You will need:

Basic dough recipe (page 15)
3 medium to large artichokes

Olive oil
1½ cups crushed tomatoes, peeled and seeded (see page 23)
2 tablespoons capers
Salt and pepper
¼ cup chopped parsley

Prepare the artichoke hearts as in the preceding recipe, keeping them in water with lemon juice until you are ready to use them. Heat a little oil in a frying pan, then add the tomatoes, the capers, and salt and pepper. After a few minutes, add the sliced artichoke hearts, well drained, and stir until they lose their raw appearance, then add the chopped parsley. Cover the pizza circles with this mixture and bake in a preheated 400° oven until the crust is browned and artichokes are tender.

Pizza with Curly Endive, No. 2 (left)
Pizza with Artichokes, No. 1 (right)

39
PIZZA WITH ARTICHOKES, No. 3

You will need:

Basic dough recipe (page 15)
3 large artichokes
Olive oil
12 cloves garlic
1 anchovy fillet, washed and mashed
3 tablespoons crushed olives
2 tablespoons capers, chopped
Pepper
¼ cup chopped parsley

Prepare the artichoke hearts as in the preceding recipes and set them aside in lemon juice and water. Heat a tablespoon of oil in a frying pan with the garlic. Crush each clove so that it gives off its flavor, but keep it whole. When the garlic has browned, remove it. Add the mashed anchovy fillet to the oil, stirring it a little, then add the olives, the capers, and finally the well-drained artichoke slices. Sprinkle with pepper and parsley. Cook the mixture for a few minutes. Pour it over the pizza dough and bake in a preheated 400° oven until golden.

40
PIZZA WITH DRIED TOMATOES

Split sun-dried tomatoes kept in glass jars come from Puglia, and can be found in Italian specialty food shops. They are conserved in green olive oil with garlic, aromatic herbs, and sometimes small bits of

Macedonian Pizza, No. 1

red pepper. There is a secret to using them: Put them on a plate in a warm oven for a few minutes; they become softer and don't dry out as quickly in cooking. You will need:

    Basic dough recipe (page 15)
    Olive oil
    1 small onion, chopped
    ½ cup marinated tomatoes, drained
    2 cups tomato sauce

Heat a little oil in a pan with the chopped onion. Add the tomatoes, revived as described above, mixing well. When they are hot, they are ready to use. Cover the dough with the tomato sauce and spoon 1 tablespoonful of the onion and dried tomatoes on each round, moisten with fresh oil, and bake in a preheated 400° oven until the dough is golden.

41
MACEDONIAN PIZZA, No. 1

You will need:

    Basic dough recipe (page 15)
    3 small zucchini
    2 tomatoes, peeled and seeded (see
        page 23)
    2 onions
    4 fleshy plums, pitted
    1 green pepper
    Olive oil
    Salt and pepper

Finely dice the zucchini, tomatoes, onions, plums, and green pepper, and mix them together in a large bowl. Slowly add a thin stream of oil till you get a rather thick mixture. If it is too watery,

drain off the excess moisture. Add salt and pepper, and spread the mixture over the pizza circles. Bake in a preheated 400° oven until the vegetables are tender and the crust is nicely browned.

42
MACEDONIAN PIZZA, No. 2

To vary the recipe above, substitute mangoes for the plums.

43
MACEDONIAN PIZZA, No. 3

The pizza can be enriched by blending into the vegetables approximately ½ cup of a fresh creamy cheese like Ricotta or Stracchino.

44
MACEDONIAN PIZZA, No. 4

Another enrichment is the addition of ½ cup of drained tuna fish to the vegetable mixture. Or add both the cheese and the tuna — the flavors go very well together.

45
PIZZA WITH BLACK TRUFFLES

You will need:
    Basic dough recipe (page 15)
    ½ cup olive oil
    8–10 cloves garlic
    4 anchovy fillets, mashed
    Pepper

Pizza with Black Truffles

melt. Pour this over the dough; there should be enough to cover the surface. Then garnish each circle with a generous amount of white truffles and bake in a preheated 400° oven until the crust is golden.

47
PIZZA WITH MUSHROOMS, No. 1

You will need:

Basic dough recipe (page 15)
2 cups sliced mushrooms
Olive oil
3 cloves garlic, finely minced
½ cup chopped parsley

Sauté the mushrooms in a little oil, add the garlic and parsley, and cook just until the mushrooms have lost their raw appearance, about 2–3 minutes. Pour the mushroom mixture over the dough and put the pizzas in a preheated 400° oven. When the dough is cooked until golden brown, the mushrooms will also be just right.

2 black truffles, each the size of a walnut, finely sliced

Make a sauce by heating the oil in a pan. Crush the cloves but keep them whole and add to the oil along with the anchovy fillets. When the garlic has browned, remove it from the oil and take the oil off the heat. Brush it over the pizza rounds and sprinkle with black pepper. Cover with thin slices of black truffle and bake in a preheated 400° oven until the crust is golden.

46
PIZZA WITH WHITE TRUFFLES AND PARMESAN

You will need:

Basic dough recipe (page 15)
Olive oil
3 cups Parmesan cheese, rather coarsely grated
2 white truffles, each the size of a walnut, finely sliced

Gently heat a small amount of oil in a pan and then add the coarsely grated cheese. Stir it so that it is coated with the oil. Do not let it

48
PIZZA WITH MUSHROOMS, No. 2

This recipe is the same as the one above except that crushed tomatoes are spread over the dough before the mushrooms are added. You will need 2–3 ripe tomatoes which should be peeled and seeded (see page 23), and then crushed and forced through a sieve. Use 2 tablespoons of tomato pulp per individual-sized pizza, add mushrooms, and bake as above.

Pizza with Mushrooms, No. 1

49
PIZZA WITH MUSHROOMS, No. 3

In this version of mushroom pizza you will need approximately 3 cups of very small cubes of eggplant. Cut the eggplant up, leaving the skin on but removing the inside pulp with seeds, salt it, and let it drain for an hour or two to remove some of the bitter taste (although some people omit this, preferring the natural flavor). Dry the cubes and fry them in olive oil. Drain them well and mix with the mushrooms that have been sautéed with garlic and parsley as in the preceding recipes. Cover the pizza with this mixture, moisten with fresh oil, and bake in a preheated 400° oven until golden.

50
PIZZA WITH MUSHROOMS, No. 4

This recipe is identical to number 3 above except that zucchini is substituted for the eggplant. You can cut the zucchini either in thin slices or into small cubes and sauté it in a small amount of oil. Drain it well and add it to the mushrooms. Cover the dough with this mixture, moisten with a little fresh olive oil, and bake as above.

51
PIZZA WITH MUSHROOMS, No. 5

This recipe calls for a special kind of Italian mushroom called *porcini* (boletus), which can be found here, dried, in Italian grocery stores. Two ounces should be ample for six pizzas. Soak them in warm water until they become soft (about 30–45 minutes), rinse thoroughly, then dry them. Slice the caps and chop up the stems. Brown them briefly in a little oil and when they have lost the first traces of rawness, add a thin stream of heavy cream, 1½ cups total. Let this cook for 2–3 minutes, then pour the mixture over the pizza circles and bake in a preheated 400° oven.

52
PIZZA WITH POTATOES AND MUSHROOMS

You will need:

Basic dough recipe (page 15)
3 medium potatoes
2 ounces dried *porcini* (boletus) mushrooms
2 tablespoons butter
6 cloves garlic, thinly sliced
¼ cup parsley, chopped
Salt and pepper

Boil the potatoes until tender, but not mushy; peel them and cut them in thin slices. Revive the *porcini* mushrooms (see recipe number 51), and slice them. Sauté the mushrooms briefly in the butter with the thinly sliced garlic, parsley, salt and pepper. On the pizza dough, first place a layer of potatoes, then 1 or 2 tablespoons of the mushrooms, and moisten the entire circle with a little olive oil. Bake in a preheated 400° oven until the dough is crisp and golden.

Pizza with Gorgonzola, No. 1

53
PIZZA WITH GORGONZOLA, No. 1

For this pizza, a milder Gorgonzola, rather than the classic Gorgonzola, works best. You will need:

Basic dough recipe (page 15)
3 cups Gorgonzola, crumbled, or Blue cheese
8–10 cloves garlic, thinly sliced or minced
Olive oil

Spread a thin layer of crumbled Gorgonzola on the pizza dough, sprinkle the minced or sliced garlic over it, moisten with olive oil and put in a preheated 400° oven until the crust is golden and the cheese has melted. Salt should not be necessary, but this depends on taste.

54
PIZZA WITH GORGONZOLA, No. 2

For garlic substitute 1 cup finely chopped onion and proceed as in version number 1.

55
PIZZA WITH GORGONZOLA, No. 3

This version calls for tomatoes. In addition to the ingredients listed

in version number 1, you will need approximately 1½ cups of crushed tomatoes or tomatoes in chunks (4–6 medium tomatoes). Sprinkle the dough with crumbled Gorgonzola as in the other versions, then the tomatoes, and a little sliced garlic. Moisten with olive oil and bake in a preheated 400° oven until the dough is golden brown and the cheese is well melted. When you take it out of the oven you can add salt or finely ground fresh pepper. I owe this recipe to Alberto Cortesi who had me try it at the Charleston restaurant in Milan.

56
PIZZA WITH APPLES AND STRACCHINO CHEESE

You need for this pizza a very soft and rather creamy cheese like Stracchino. A substitute might be farmer's cheese or Ricotta. You will need:

Basic dough recipe (page 15)
1½ cups Stracchino or other mild soft cheese, crumbled
3 medium apples, preferably Golden Delicious, chopped very fine
Olive oil

Roll out the dough until very thin. Mix the chopped apple in with the cheese and spread it over the dough. Moisten with a little oil and bake in a preheated 400° oven until the apple has softened and the crust has turned golden.

57
PIZZA WITH APPLES AND GORGONZOLA

If you like an apple and cheese pizza with a stronger flavor, try the contrast of a slightly acidic, green apple with Gorgonzola, the rich butter-flavored kind with unexpected sharp bites. As in the preceding recipe, mix the finely chopped apples with crumbled Gorgonzola and spread over the pizza circles, moisten with oil, and bake in a preheated 400° oven until the apple has softened and the crust has turned golden.

Three-Cheese Pizza (above)
Pizza with Apples and Stracchino Cheese (left)

58
THREE-CHEESE PIZZA

You will need:

Basic dough recipe (page 15)
1 cup Scamorza or Mozzarella cheese, grated
1 cup Fontina or Gruyère cheese, grated
1 cup Provolone or Pecorino cheese, grated
Salt and pepper
Olive oil

Mix the cheeses together and distribute over the rounds of pizza, sprinkle with salt and pepper, and moisten with oil. Bake in a preheated 400° oven until the crust is golden and the cheese has melted and slightly browned.

Another good combination might be Parmesan, Mozzarella and Gruyère, but you can enjoy yourself thinking up others.

Sometimes the grated cheese is first melted just a little in some butter with salt and pepper. A good trick is to dissolve a tablespoon of flour in 2 tablespoons of milk and stir this into the cheese, allowing to cook over low heat for several minutes. This forms a creamy mass that can be poured over the pizza dough and then baked.

59
FOUR-CHEESE PIZZA

This recipe is the same as above except that you combine four cheeses instead of three. You can try various combinations, for example, adding Gorgonzola to the three mentioned above. The most buttery Gorgonzola is the best, since it tolerates the heat the best and melts smoothly.

60
FIVE-CHEESE PIZZA

Again the recipe is similar to the previous ones except for the num-

ber of cheeses. A good combination of five cheeses might be Mozzarella, Provolone, Fontina, Swiss, and Gorgonzola. But there are many possibilities including Parmesan, Caciocavallo, Pecorino, or Romano.

61
PIZZA WITH SCAMORZA OR MOZZARELLA AND POTATOES

You will need:

Basic dough recipe (page 15)
3 medium potatoes
¾ pound cheese, either Mozzarella or Scamorza
6 anchovy fillets, rinsed and chopped
Olive oil
Pepper

Boil the potatoes until tender, but not mushy; peel them and cut them into thin slices. Cut the cheese into thin slices as well and spread potatoes and cheese over the pizza in alternating layers. On top sprinkle the pieces of anchovy, moisten with the oil, and sprinkle with a little coarsely ground pepper. Bake in a preheated 400° oven until the crust is golden.

62
PIZZA WITH TALEGGIO CHEESE

Taleggio is a semi-soft, somewhat pungent cheese made from cow's milk. You can substitute any

soft creamy cheese. You will need approximately 3 cups of Taleggio or other cheese, crumbled over the pizza circles. Moisten them with oil and bake in a preheated 400° oven.

A few tablespoons of finely chopped onion sprinkled over the cheese before baking give this pizza a richer flavor.

Pizza alla Capogna

63
PIZZA ALLA CAPOGNA

This is an adaptation of a recipe created by one of the best chefs I know, Pino Capogna. You will need:

Basic dough recipe (page 15)
2 tablespoons horseradish
2 tablespoons soybean oil
2 tablespoons vinegar
¾ pound Ricotta cheese
Olive oil
¼ pound Mascarpone or cream cheese mixed with a little cream to make it softer

Mix the horseradish with the oil and vinegar and let it marinate for 2 hours. Then drain off the oil and vinegar and mix the horseradish with the Ricotta and Mascarpone or cream cheese. Mix them well to obtain a smooth and homogenous mixture, adding olive oil little by little as necessary. Cover the pizzas with this and bake in a pre-heated 400° oven.

64
PESTO PIZZA

You will need:

Basic dough recipe (page 15)
1 cup fresh basil leaves
6 cloves garlic
⅓ cup Pecorino or Parmesan cheese
⅓ cup pine nuts (optional)
Coarse salt
¾ cup olive oil

The pesto should be the classic one. Crush the basil together with the garlic and a pinch of coarse salt (which helps to preserve the green color of the basil) in a mortar or food processor, then add the oil little by little until you get a well-blended puree, and finally add the cheese and the pine nuts (some don't consider the latter necessary while others think them obligatory).

Put the pizza circles, moistened only with a little oil, in a preheated 400° oven. When they are half-baked, take them out and cover them generously with the pesto and then put them back in to finish cooking.

65
PIZZA WITH ONIONS, RICOTTA, AND GORGONZOLA

You will need:

Basic dough recipe (page 15)
3 medium onions, finely chopped
1½ cups Ricotta cheese
1½ cups Gorgonzola or Blue cheese

Pizza with Onions, Ricotta, and Gorgonzola

Salt
Olive oil

Beat the onion, Ricotta and Gorgonzola together, adding a little salt and enough oil to bind and soften the mixture. Cover the pizza dough with this mixture and bake in a preheated 400° oven until the cheese has melted and the crust is golden.

You can use milk instead of oil, and you can also add finely chopped celery to either the milk or oil version.

66
PIZZA WITH CICINIELLI

Cicinielli are a tiny fish, virtually transparent, found around Naples. Since they are unlikely to be found in this country, we include this recipe more for its interest than as an actual suggestion. The pizza dough is covered with a layer of these tiny fish. Chopped or sliced garlic, a pinch of oregano, salt and pepper are added, and the whole thing is moistened with green olive oil before baking.

67
PIZZA WITH CLAMS, No. 1

You will need:

Basic dough recipe (page 15)
36–48 clams (littlenecks or cherry-stones are about the right size)
4–6 medium tomatoes, peeled and seeded (see page 23), chopped, crushed or in wedges
Salt and pepper
Oregano

Place the scrubbed clams in a pan over low heat and cover. When they have opened, remove the meat, filter the water that is released and set it aside. Spread the tomatoes over the pizza rounds, sprinkle with salt, pepper, and a pinch of oregano, and bake in a preheated 400° oven until the dough is browned. When the pizza is ready, cover with the clams, moisten with a little of the clam water, and serve immediately.

68
PIZZA WITH CLAMS, No. 2

The recipe is the same as described above, except that the tomatoes are eliminated. The circles are baked simply moistened with a little olive oil, a sprinkling of oregano, and a pinch of salt and pepper. After baking, each circle is garnished with the clams, pre-

Pizza with Clams, No. 1

pared as described in recipe 67, and served immediately.

69
PIZZA WITH MUSSELS

Many people prefer mussels, because of their delicacy, to clams. You will need 3 quarts, which must be carefully scrubbed and bearded. The procedure is exactly the same as with clams (see above), both in the version with tomatoes and the version without. But the flavor of the tomatoes can easily predominate, so if you use them, you might wish to use less. When the dough has baked, garnish with the mussels and moisten with a little left-over mussel juice.

70
PIZZA WITH SEA DATES

This is another tiny shellfish not found in this country, but any small

shellfish might be substituted, including tiny scallops. If you use scallops, sauté them briefly in a little olive oil to which you have added finely chopped garlic, then follow the recipe for clams or mussels above. You would need approximately 1½ pounds of scallops.

71
PIZZA WITH SHRIMP OR PRAWNS

You will need approximately 2 pounds of small shrimp, boiled and shelled. Follow the procedure in recipe 67.

72
PIZZA WITH MIXED SEAFOOD

This can be made with all kinds of seafood, not only those already mentioned but also squid and others. The squid should be cleaned, cut up in bite-size pieces, and sautéed briefly, then added with the other ingredients after baking as described in recipe 67. You will need about three cups of prepared seafood altogether. A good combination would be shrimp, squid, mussels, and clams, but any combination could work.

73
PIZZA WITH OYSTERS

This is also a recent invention. You will need:

Basic dough recipe (page 15)
Olive oil
Salt
30–36 oysters
1 lemon

Moisten the circles of dough with a little olive olive, sprinkle with salt, and bake them in a preheated 400° oven until they are golden brown. While they bake, prepare the oysters. Steam them open (see recipe 67), place them on a plate, and gently squeeze a little lemon juice over them. When the dough is baked, cover it with oysters and sprinkle with a little freshly ground pepper.

74
PIZZA WITH FRESH ANCHOVIES

This is very similar to the more traditional pizza with *cicinielli*. You will need:

Basic dough recipe (page 15)
12–15 fresh anchovies (preferably small ones)
4–6 cloves garlic, sliced or chopped
Olive oil
Salt and pepper

Place several anchovies on each pizza round and sprinkle garlic over them. Moisten the rounds with olive oil, sprinkle with salt and pepper, and bake in a preheated 400° oven.

The anchovies are even better if marinated in a little oil with garlic, salt, and pepper for an hour or two (no vinegar or lemon should be used, as it leaves an acidic taste). Pour the whole mixture over the pizza and bake.

A good substitute in this country might be smelts.

75
PIZZA WITH FRESH SARDINES

The recipe is similar to the one above for fresh anchovies, but in some versions sieved tomato pulp is spread over the dough before adding the well-cleaned and deboned sardines, either fresh or tinned. You will need approximately 20–30 in all, depending on size.

76
PIZZA WITH SQUID

You will need:

Basic dough recipe (page 15)
1½ pounds cleaned squid
1 small onion, finely chopped
2 tablespoons parsley, finely chopped
3 tablespoons oil
Salt and pepper

Cut the tentacles off the cleaned squid and divide them, and then cut the body in rings. Make a *soffritto* by sautéing the onion in the oil, then add the parsley. Let this cook a few minutes, then add the body of the squid cut in rings and the tentacles, salt, and pepper. This mixture is spread over the dough and baked in a preheated 400° oven until golden.

77
PIZZA WITH FRESH FISH EGGS

When they can be found, fresh fish eggs, or roe, are like manna for any kind of cooking. You will need:

Basic dough recipe (page 15)
¾ cup chopped onion
½ pound fish eggs
Olive oil

Spread 2 tablespoons of chopped onion on each pizza round, and then divide the fish eggs among them. Moisten with olive oil and bake in a preheated 400° oven until the crust is golden.

78
PIZZA WITH SEAWEED

This came from a spaghetti recipe of my friend Emilio Regonaschi. Fresh seaweed can occasionally be found in fish stores. You will need:

Basic dough recipe (page 15)
4–6 cups fresh seaweed
1 pound Gorgonzola cheese
Grappa or brandy

Wash the seaweed well, chop it up, and then either puree in a blender, or force through a sieve. Mix the pulp with the Gorgonzola cheese and grappa to taste. Spread this mixture over the pizza circles and bake in a preheated 400° oven until golden.

You can also use dry seaweed, which can be found in stores carrying Japanese products or other foreign or specialty stores. Soak the dry seaweed in warm water, drain, and proceed as above.

79
PIZZA WITH APPLES AND SHRIMP

The combination of shrimp and apples, a classic antipasto, also makes a delicious pizza. You will need:

Basic dough recipe (page 15)
2 pounds small shrimp
3 tart green apples, cut into very small cubes
Olive oil

Clean, shell, and cut the shrimp into small pieces. Spread the chopped apples over the circles, approximately 3 tablespoons per small pizza, then add the shrimp, moisten with oil, and bake in a preheated 400° oven until the crust has turned a golden brown.

80
PIZZA WITH SMOKED HERRING

Smoked herring, cleaned and coarsely chopped, takes the place of salted anchovies in this recipe for Roman-style pizza. You will need:

Basic dough recipe (page 15)
¾ pound herring, boned and coarsely chopped
4–6 medium tomatoes, peeled, seeded and cut in wedges (as on page 23)
1 pound Mozzarella cheese, sliced
Olive oil
Pepper

Pizza with Seaweed

It is a good idea to let the herring soak in milk for a few hours before chopping so that it will be less salty. Meanwhile, roll out thin rounds of dough and when the herring is ready, spread over the dough first the tomatoes, then the Mozzarella, and last the pieces of herring. Moisten with olive oil and bake in a preheated 400° oven until the crust is golden and the tomatoes are soft. When it is done, sprinkle with coarsely ground pepper.

In some versions, the tomato is omitted.

81
PIZZA WITH SMOKED EEL

The recipe is the same as described in recipe 80, but eels are substituted for the herring.

82
PIZZA WITH SMOKED SALMON

You will need:

Basic dough recipe (page 15)
¼–½ pound smoked salmon, cut into small bits
1 small onion, finely chopped

Mint
Olive oil

On very thin rounds of dough, spread the smoked salmon and chopped onion, mixing them a little. Sprinkle with a little fresh or dried mint and moisten with oil. Bake in a preheated 400° oven until the crust is golden.

83
PIZZA WITH CAVIAR

This is quite expensive, of course, but extraordinary if you try

it. Generously spread the caviar and a little chopped onion over a very thin round of dough, sprinkle with a tablespoon of finely chopped parsley, moisten with oil and bake in a preheated 400° oven until the crust is golden.

84
PIZZA WITH RED CAVIAR

The recipe is the same as for pizza with the classic caviar, but you can, if it pleases your palate, add a bit more onion.

85
PIZZA WITH TUNA FISH, No. 1

You will need:

Basic dough recipe (page 15)
8-ounce can of tuna fish
1 medium onion, chopped
Fresh basil leaves
Olive oil

Crumble up a can of good-quality tuna fish in a bowl after you have drained off the liquid. Mix in the onion and spread it over the rounds of dough. Garnish with a few fresh basil leaves, moisten with

Pizza with Tuna Fish, No. 1 (above)
Pizza with Smoked Salmon (left)

a little oil, and bake in a preheated 400° oven until the crust is golden.

86
PIZZA WITH TUNA FISH, No. 2

The recipe is the same as above but you can add ½ cup of chopped black or green olives or chopped celery to the tuna fish before it is baked.

87
PIZZA WITH TUNA FISH, No. 3

This recipe is similar to the preceding ones with tuna. But in this version, only add ½ cup of chopped celery to the crumbled tuna fish and omit the other ingredients. Spread it on the dough and moisten with a little olive oil. Bake as above.

88
PIZZA WITH TUNA FISH, No. 4

Make the classic *soffritto* by sautéing 1 small chopped onion in 2 tablespoons oil, then add one tomato, peeled, seeded, and chopped, and let this cook together a few minutes. Add drained tuna fish to this mixture, stirring it a little to break it up. Spread the mixture over the dough and bake in a preheated 400° oven until the crust is golden brown.

You can also add a tablespoon of chopped celery or capers.

89
PIZZA WITH TUNA FISH AND RICOTTA

You will need:

Basic dough recipe (page 15)
1 pound Ricotta cheese
8 ounces tuna fish, well drained
Olive oil
Onion juice
Pepper

Work the Ricotta and tuna together until they are well mixed, then slowly add enough oil so that you have a smooth mixture. Add onion juice and pepper to taste. Cover the pizza round with this mixture and bake in a preheated 400° oven until golden.

90
PIZZA WITH BOTTARGA

Bottarga are the dried eggs of a fish found in Italy. They are pressed and dried in the sun and end up looking a little like salami. Tuna *bottarga* also exists; it is saltier but also appetizing. Smoked cod roe could be substituted in this country. For the pizzas you will need:

Basic dough recipe (page 15)
¾ cup chopped onion
½ pound *bottarga*, grated
Olive oil

Sprinkle each round of dough with chopped onion and grated *bottarga*. Moisten with olive oil and bake in a preheated 400° oven until the crust is golden.

You can also cover the circle with slices of Mozzarella, then the *bottarga*, moisten with olive oil and bake.

91
PIZZA WITH SNAILS

You will need:

Basic dough recipe (page 15)
3 cans (7½ ounce) snails

¾ cup white wine
1 small onion, finely chopped
1 small tomato, peeled and seeded (see page 23) and finely chopped
3 tablespoons olive oil
Salt and pepper

Marinate the snails in ½ cup of the wine for an hour. Make a *soffritto* by sautéing the onion and tomato in the olive oil with a sprinkling of salt and pepper. Add the remaining ¼ cup of white wine. Drain and add the snails, letting them cook for 2–3 minutes. Cover the circles of dough with this mixture and bake in a preheated 400° oven until snails and dough are done.

92
PIZZA WITH HAM, No. 1

The difficulty in preparing this pizza, which is liked by so many, especially in northern Italy, is that the ham dries out when cooked in the oven at high temperatures. Therefore it is a good idea to cut it in small strips, thick enough to include some of the fatty part, if possible. You will need:

Basic dough recipe (page 15)
½ pound fatty ham or prosciutto
2 cups Mozzarella cheese, cubed or in slices
Olive oil

Arrange the ham on the dough, cover with the Mozzarella, and moisten with a little oil. Bake in a preheated 400° oven until the crust is golden and the cheese has melted.

93
PIZZA WITH HAM, No. 2

In this version, you can substitute Fontina or Bel Paese or other soft cheese you like for the Mozzarella in recipe 92, and then add 1 cup chopped black or green olives.

94
PIZZA WITH HAM, No. 3

In this version spread sieved tomato pulp over the dough. You will need approximately 2 cups of peeled, seeded and chopped tomatoes (see page 23), passed through a sieve or put in the blender. Then add the ham, taking care that it retains some of its fat, and the Mozzarella cubes, and moisten with a little olive oil. Bake in a preheated 400° oven until golden.

95
PIZZA WITH FRESH SAUSAGE

This recipe is similar to recipe 92, using Mozzarella or another fresh soft cheese. In this version you can use either fresh or dry sausage, although it should not be too dry. Proceed as in recipe 92.

96
PIZZA WITH FRANKS

Slices of frankfurters are used in this recipe. They are best if they are first boiled and peeled. You will need approximately 12 franks, although this will vary with size. Proceed as in recipe 92.

Pizza with Ham, No. 1

97
PIZZA WITH POTATOES AND FRESH SAUSAGE

You will need:

Basic dough recipe (page 15)
3–4 medium potatoes
½ pound fresh pork sausage
Olive oil
Salt

Boil the potatoes until tender, but not mushy, then peel them and cut them into thin slices. Crumble the sausage or cut it into rounds. Put a layer of potatoes over the dough, moisten with a little oil, sprinkle with salt, and garnish with the sausage. Moisten with a little more oil and bake in a preheated 400° oven until the crust is golden and the sausage has cooked.

98
PIZZA WITH COTECHINO SAUSAGE AND EGG SAUCE

Cotechino sausages are fresh, coarsely ground pork sausage with a thick skin. They are usually about 8 inches long and 2½ inches in diameter. Any coarsely ground pork sausage can be substituted. You will need:

Basic dough recipe (page 15)
1 pound *cotechino* sausage or other pork sausage
1 pound Ricotta or other fresh cheese
6 eggs
3 tablespoons of tuna
Olive oil
Lemon juice

Cook the *cotechino* sausage over low heat in a covered skillet with ¼ inch of water in the bottom for 20–30 minutes. Cut it in slices, neither very thick nor very thin. Spread the cheese generously over the dough and put the slices of sausage on top. Bake in a preheated 400° oven until the crust is golden.

Meanwhile, prepare a sauce by beating together the eggs and the tuna, adding oil until the mixture is creamy. At the end add a few drops of lemon juice. When the pizza is cooked, bring it to the front of the oven, cover with the sauce, and remove it from the oven. The heat should cause the eggs to set. Serve immediately.

99
PIZZA ALLA CRISTOFORO

This pizza was the idea of Cristoforo Adesini, a true pizza lover. Cristoforo owns a restaurant in

Pizza with Potatoes and Fresh Sausage

Milan, in the Via Napo Torriani, where pizzamakers and other friends get together to experiment with new recipes, often with brilliant results. You will need:

Basic dough recipe (page 15)
1 pound Mozzarella cheese, sliced
¾ cup thick tomato sauce
1½ cups grated Pecorino or Romano cheese
1 small pepperoni, sliced thin
24 thin asparagus tips, cooked al dente
Fresh basil leaves, wiped clean with a dry cloth
Olive oil

Roll out the dough so that it is especially thin and will become crispy when baked. Cover it with slices of Mozzarella thin enough that they will melt completely during cooking, then spread a tablespoon or two of tomato sauce on each pizza and sprinkle the Pecorino on top. Garnish with the pepperoni, 6–8 slices per pizza, the asparagus tips (4 per pizza), and the basil leaves. Moisten each one with oil and bake in a preheated 400° oven until the dough is crisp and golden.

This pizza, although it is very rich, has ingredients that go together very well.

100
PIZZA WITH SAGE

Speaking of Cristoforo's pizza I am reminded of another experiment from the Torriani restaurant.

Pizza alla Cristoforo

This idea came from the piz- zamaker Franco Genna.

Basic dough recipe (page 15)
1 pound Mozzarella cheese, sliced very
thin
6 tablespoons ketchup
¾ cup fresh sage, minced
Olive oil

Roll out very thin circles of dough and over them spread the Mozzarella, and instead of the usual tomato sauce, spread a spoonful of ketchup on each circle. On top sprinkle a generous amount of fresh minced sage, moisten with oil, and bake in a preheated 400° oven until cheese has completely melted and the crust is golden.

101
PIZZA WITH PANCETTA, No. 1

Pancetta is a fatty bacon-like roll which can be seen in the picture on page 64. Thin-sliced bacon can be substituted, although the flavor will not be the same. You will need:

Basic dough recipe (page 15)
1 pound *pancetta* or fatty bacon, sliced
thin
1½ cups grated Pecorino or Romano
cheese
Olive oil

Cut the *pancetta* or bacon to separate the fat from the lean. Chop the fat very finely and cut the lean into small pieces. Scatter the fat over the base of the circle first so that it forms a very thin layer

covering the bottom, leaving a small margin around the edge. On top, distribute the lean part evenly and then sprinkle with the cheese, moisten with oil, and bake in a preheated 400° oven until the crust is golden and the pizza is cooked through.

102
PIZZA WITH PANCETTA, No. 2

For this slightly more elaborate version you will need:

Basic dough recipe (page 15)
1 pound *pancetta* or fatty bacon
Olive oil
3 cups chopped onion
1 cup tomato pulp, made from peeled, seeded and chopped tomatoes (see page 23) passed through a sieve, or canned tomatoes
Salt and pepper

Cut the *pancetta* or bacon in small cubes. Put a very little oil in a skillet and add the *pancetta*. Let it brown a little, then drain and keep warm. Meanwhile, in another pan, sauté the onions in a little oil until they are translucent, then add the tomato pulp, salt, and pepper and let this cook gently for a few minutes. Finally, pour it over the dough, sprinkle with the *pancetta* and bake in a preheated 400° oven until the crust is golden.

For variation, you can add chopped black or green olives.

Pizza with Pancetta, No. 2

103
PIZZA WITH HOG JOWLS

This unusual pizza is made with hog jowls. Hog jowls are cured and smoked like bacon and found mostly in the South. You will need:

Basic dough recipe (page 15)
Olive oil
8 ounces hog jowls, cut in thin strips
1½ cups Pecorino or Romano cheese, grated

Moisten the dough with a little oil, then scatter 3 tablespoons of hog jowls per pizza over the dough. Cover with a sprinkling of cheese and bake in a preheated 400° oven until the crust is golden and the cheese has melted.

104
PIZZA WITH PORK RINDS

You will need:

Basic dough recipe (page 15)
1 pound pork rinds
1½ cups good tomato sauce
Pepper

The pork rinds are cleaned, scraped to get rid of the little hairs, and cut into little pieces or strips and boiled until they are very soft. Add them to the tomato sauce and cover the pizza dough with this mixture. Sprinkle with freshly ground pepper and bake in a preheated 400° oven until the crust is golden and the pork rinds are crisp.

105
PIZZA ALLA FRANCO

This was an original creation of Franco Genna, a Sicilian pizzamaker living in Milan. You will need:

Basic dough recipe (page 15)
1 pound Mozzarella cheese, cut in slices
6 tablespoons of a good-quality sharp mustard
½ pound *pancetta* or bacon cut into cubes
Olive oil

Roll out the dough into thin circles. Arrange the slices of Mozzarella over each one, then spread with a spoonful of mustard, scatter the *pancetta* or bacon on top, moisten with oil, and bake in a preheated 400° oven until the crust is browned.

106
PIZZA WITH CHICKEN LIVERS

You will need:

Basic dough recipe (page 15)
1 pound chicken livers
Olive oil
8–10 cloves of garlic
Salt and pepper
½ cup chopped parsley

Clean the chicken livers and cut into small pieces. Sauté them briefly in a little oil with the garlic and salt and pepper. Pour this over the circles of dough, sprinkle with parsley, and bake in a preheated 400° oven until the dough is crisp. After the pizzas are baked, grind coarse black pepper over all.

107
PIZZA WITH TRIPE

You will need:

Basic dough recipe (page 15)
1 pound tripe
1½ cups tomato sauce
1½ cups grated Parmesan or Romano cheese

Clean and wash the tripe and boil it so that it loses its fattiness. Then cut it into rather short strips. Heat the tomato sauce and add the tripe to it, letting it cook for 2–3 minutes. Cover the pizza circles with this mixture, sprinkle with grated cheese, and bake in a preheated 400° oven until the crust is browned.

108
PIZZA WITH PROSCIUTTO AND FIGS

You will need:

Basic dough recipe (page 15)
2 dozen ripe figs, cut into pieces
½ pound proscuitto, cut into strips containing both fat and lean meat
Olive oil

Roll out the dough into thin circles. Arrange a layer of figs over them and then cover with strips of prosciutto. Moisten with oil and bake in a preheated 400° oven until the dough is golden.

This may seen like a strange combination to some, but figs were often used in sauces in olden times with good results. Others will have already tasted prosciutto and figs as an antipasto. Try it.

109
PIZZA WITH PEPPERS AND FIGS

I mentioned above that figs were common in olden days. The Latin writer Apicius, for example, who left us the only more or less complete Roman cookbook, gives us many recipes where figs were part of sauces and stews, often replacing onions. A famous recipe in ancient Rome was *jecur ficatum*, which was liver with figs, a dish in which the figs were sautéed in a little oil and strips of liver, herbs, and spices were added.

History aside, for the pizza with peppers and figs, you will need:

Basic dough recipe (page 15)
24 ripe figs, cut into pieces
Olive oil
4 medium green peppers, chopped

Spread the green peppers over the dough, moisten with a little oil, and then garnish with the fig meat. Bake in a preheated 400° oven until the crust is golden.

To vary the flavor, you can add a little chopped celery to the peppers.

Pizza with Green Peppers and Figs

110
FOUR SEASONS PIZZA, No. 1

You will need:

Basic dough recipe (page 15)
3 cloves garlic
6–12 anchovy fillets
¾ cup black olives, chopped and pitted
¾ cup clams or other seafood
⅓ cup tomato pulp
¾ cup Mozzarella cheese, grated
Olive oil

Cut off a small section from the dough before you roll it out. Use this to make two cords for each pizza, which will cross and divide it into four sections on top. In each section, put different ingredients, taking care that none of the ingredients clash with each other. For example, in one quarter, you might put garlic, anchovies, and a little oil; in another, black olives and anchovies; in the third quarter, the clams; and in the last quarter, tomatoes, Mozzarella and again anchovies. Bake it in a preheated 400° oven until the crust is golden.

111
FOUR SEASONS PIZZA, No. 2

This is identical to the recipe above, except that in the first section you put clams; in the second quarter you put Mozzarella and tomatoes; in the third, garlic, anchovies, and oil; and in the fourth, artichoke hearts preserved in oil or frozen and cooked (in the latter case, drain them and moisten them with a little oil first), or a mixture of vegetables in oil.

112
FOUR SEASONS PIZZA, No. 3

All kinds of pizzas can be made using the methods described in recipe 110. One variation might use Mozzarella and tomato in one section; mushrooms in another; olives and capers in a third; and in the last, fresh crumbled sausage, ham, or prosciutto mixed with small cubes of Mozzarella.

Four Seasons Pizza, No. 1

113
PIZZA AL RAGU

I owe this idea to the artist Angelo Cattaneo, who does very elegant abstract works but in the kitchen remains very close to the traditional methods of his native Cremona. This pizza calls for a very fresh ragu, with more vegeta-

bles than meat. You will need:

Basic dough recipe (page 15)
4 tablespoons olive oil
1 medium onion, chopped
2 stalks celery, chopped
1 large carrot, finely chopped
Salt and pepper
6 ounces ground beef

Heat the oil and add the chopped onion. Cook until the onion becomes translucent, then add the celery, carrots, salt, and pepper. Let the vegetables cook a few minutes and add the beef. Let the meat brown and then divide this mixture among the six pizza circles. Moisten with a little oil and bake in a preheated 400° oven until the crust is golden.

For a red version, add 1 medium tomato, peeled and seeded (see page 23) and passed through a sieve, to the ragu after you add the meat.

114
PIZZA WITH PLANTAINS

This recipe was born in South America, where the Italian pizza has been successfully adapted to local products. You will need:

Basic dough recipe (page 15)
Lard or oil
4 plantains (the best kind are the small green ones)

Make a very thin crust from the dough and brush it with a light film of lard or oil. Cut the plantains into thin slices and flatten them a bit

with a wooden spatula. (In some Latin American countries they are fried first, just as we do with potatoes.) Then cover the dough with a generous layer of plantain slices and put in a preheated 400° oven until the crust is golden.

115
PIZZA WITH PINEAPPLE, No. 1

This recipe was also originated in South America by Italian pizza-makers looking for recipes that would satisfy local taste. It is rather sweet but quite pleasing. You will need:

Basic dough recipe (page 14)
1 fresh pineapple, cut into tiny pieces or crushed (approximately 2 cups)
Palm or other light oil

Roll out the dough so that it is very thin, spread a generous amount of fresh pineapple over it, moisten with palm oil, and bake in a preheated 400° oven until golden. I owe this recipe to my friend Antonio Primiceri.

116
PIZZA WITH PINEAPPLE, No. 2

In this version spread the fresh pineapple over the thin dough, then mix in soft crumbled Gorgonzola cheese and moisten with a light vegetable oil. Bake in a preheated 400° oven until golden. The pineapple and Gorgonzola create an elegant sweet-sour taste.

117
PIZZA WITH RED CURRANTS

In this recipe, substitute red currants for the pineapple. Then follow the directions for either version of Pizza with Pineapple, according to preference.

118
PIZZA WITH STRAWBERRIES

In this recipe, substitute strawberries for the pineapple and follow either variation 1 or 2. Be sure the strawberries are not too ripe.

119
PIZZA WITH KIWIS

The kiwi is a little fruit, brown and furry on the outside and bright green inside. They say it is richer in vitamin C than ten lemons. It comes from New Zealand and New

Pizza with Pineapple, No. 2

Zealanders are sometimes called kiwi (which, incidentally, means "small mouse"). The kiwi is an excellent fruit, used fresh in fruit salads and other dishes and in this case it can substitute for the pineapple or currants of the preceding recipes.

120 PIZZA WITH AVOCADO

The avocado is another exotic fruit whose meat can be used in place of the pineapple. The avocado, however, has a rather mild flavor and needs to be livened up. You might mix it with the currants or strawberries, for example.

121 PIZZA WITH HEARTS OF PALM

Another recipe as we visit pizza around the world. Sprinkle chopped onions and pieces of hearts of palm over the dough, moisten with oil, add salt and pepper, and bake in a preheated 400° oven until the crust is golden. For a red version, you can put crushed tomatoes on the dough first, then add the other ingredients.

122 PIZZA WITH WALNUTS OR HAZELNUTS

Typically, Stracchino or Mascarpone are the cheeses eaten with nuts in Italy. In this recipe you will need:

Basic dough recipe (page 15)
1½ cups walnuts or hazelnuts, chopped
1 pound Mascarpone, Stracchino, or whipped cream cheese to which a little cream is added
Olive or walnut oil

Mix the nuts with the cheese, moisten the dough with oil, and spread some of the cheese and nut mixture over it. Add a little more oil and bake in a preheated 400° oven until the crust is golden.

123 PIZZA WITH SPAGHETTI

This may seem like a truly excessive idea, but when my friend Emilio Regonaschi presented it as a tribute at a large international gathering of pizzamakers, it met with great success. You will need:

Basic dough recipe (page 15)
¾ pound spaghetti
Spaghetti sauce: tomato, ragu, or clam, as you prefer
Oil or lard

Prepare the pizza dough and brush it with a little lard or oil. Meanwhile have a pot of boiling water ready for the spaghetti. Just after you put the dough into the oven, drop the spaghetti into the boiling water. It should be half cooked when the pizza is nearly ready. Drain the spaghetti and add the sauce of your choice to it.

Cover the pizza circles with the spaghetti and sauce just before the dough is completely cooked, and put them back in the oven for no more the 2–3 minutes. Remember that the heat of the oven is much greater than the pot of boiling water, so 2–3 minutes is enough for the pasta and the pizza dough to finish cooking and for their flavors and aromas to blend.

Actually this pizza is not a brand-new creation. The great comic actor Gilberto Govi loved it and always ordered it when he went to a local pizzeria in Imperia. Some of the details may be slightly different, but the recipe is basically the same as reported.

124 CALZONE

Calzone is most probably the natural evolution of the pizza. The circle is more generously filled and then folded over and the edges are pressed together to keep the filling inside. The pizza can be held on paper and eaten with your hands, but not so the calzone. It requires at least a plate, a knife to cut it, and a fork to eat it with. This creates a big gap between the pizza and the calzone, both gastronomically and psychologically speaking, even

though they are very similar in taste.

You can use either purchased bread dough or you can make your own. To make your own, enough for 6 servings, you will need:

3⅓ cups flour, approximately
1 cube (⅔ ounce) compressed yeast dissolved in ½ cup lukewarm water
Salt
2 tablespoons olive oil

Add an additional cup of water to the yeast mixture. Add the salt and the oil and start adding the flour until the dough becomes too stiff to stir. Turn out on a floured board and continue kneading in the rest of the flour until you have a smooth, elastic dough. Let this rest under a cloth for at least an hour. Knead it as with pizza dough (page 15) until it can be easily rolled out.

Meanwhile, prepare the filling. You will need:

1½ cups Ricotta cheese
1 cup Mozzarella cheese, cubed
1 cup sausage, salami, or ham, cubed
2 tablespoons Pecorino or ·Romano cheese, grated
4 eggs

Mix the first four ingredients and 3 of the eggs together so that they are neither too dry nor too moist. Then divide the dough into six parts and roll each one out into a circle about ¹⁄₁₆ inch thick. Divide the filling among the circles, placing it on one half of each circle.

Calzone

Fold the free side over and firmly press the edges together. Beat the remaining egg and use to paint the surface of the calzone. Place on a greased baking sheet and bake in a preheated 400° oven until golden.

125
POOR MAN'S CALZONE

The poor man's version is still popular in southern Italy, the Magna Grecia of ancient times. The recipe for the dough is the same as the preceding recipe. For filling you will need:

1 pound fresh spinach
Olive oil
⅓ cup black olives, pitted and chopped
Salt
⅛ teaspoon red pepper
1½ cups Ricotta cheese

Boil the spinach, drain, and chop it up well. Sauté it briefly in a little oil with the olives, salt, and red pepper. Mix with the ricotta and proceed as in recipe 124. Other versions add a few thin slices of soft cheese, like Mozzarella.

126
CALZONE, THE OLD-FASHIONED WAY

In this traditional version, the stuffing is made with Ricotta and greens—spinach, beet greens or

whatever you like—prepared as in the previous recipe. The boiled and chopped greens are sautéed with ⅓ cup of raisins, first revived in a little warm water and drained, and ⅓ cup of pine nuts in place of the olives, salt and pepper.

127
CALZONE WITH COTECHINO SAUSAGE

This version is from the Emilia region and it has recently become popular. Make a filling with 2½ cups Mozzarella, cubed, 8 ounces of cooked *cotechino* (see recipe 98) or other coarsely ground pork sausage, cubed or crumbled, and 3 beaten eggs. Then proceed as in recipe 124.

128
CALZONE WITH FISH

This stuffing is made with fish (for example, sardines, fresh anchovies or mackerel), which are first cleaned, then floured and fried in a little oil. They are then drained well on absorbent towels. The meat is moistened with fresh oil and a little chopped parsley is added to them. You can also use various fish togther, fresh or canned, or shellfish. You will need about ¾ pound fresh fish or 8 ounces canned. Be sure to chop them up well before mixing them together. Then assemble calzone as in master recipe 124.

129
GREEN CALZONE

This is jokingly called "green" calzone because it is filled with greens, but it can also be filled with vegetables of other colors. The usual fillings include spinach, beet greens, escarole, zucchini, onions, peppers, or whatever you have available.

You will need a total of 6 cups for 6 calzones. The vegetables are cleaned, boiled, chopped, and then sautéed briefly in a skillet with a little oil, salt, pepper, and chopped parsley. They should stay on the *al dente* or crisp side. Drain them well and mix with 1 cup of crumbled fresh cheese, such as Ricotta or cottage cheese. You can also add a few tablespoons of grated Parmesan cheese. Add just enough olive oil to bind the mixture well, then fill the circles of dough, seal, and bake as in master recipe 124.

130
CALZONE WITH ONIONS

This filling is made with a large amount of onions. For 6 servings you will need:

Basic calzone dough (see recipe 124)

Green Calzone

6–8 medium onions, chopped or sliced
Olive oil
6 anchovy fillets
1 cup tomatoes, peeled, seeded and crushed (see page 23)
Salt and pepper
1 cup grated Pecorino or Romano cheese

Sauté the onions in oil with the anchovies and the tomatoes. Add salt and pepper to taste. When the mixture is thoroughly mixed and well cooked, remove from the heat and add the cheese. Fill the six calzone circles as in the master recipe, 124, moistening each one with a little oil before folding them over. Bake in a preheated 400° oven until golden.

You can add ¼ cup of raisins, previously soaked in warm water to revive them, but in that case it is better to eliminate the cheese. You can also add 2 ounces of Parmesan to the Pecorino or Romano, mixing them together before adding them to the other ingredients.

131
CALZONE WITH ESCAROLE

Follow master recipe 124 for the calzone dough. For the filling you will need:

6 tablespoons olive oil
2–3 cloves garlic, crushed

4 anchovy fillets, chopped
6 cups escarole
2–3 tablespoons capers
¼ cup chopped and pitted black olives

Heat the oil and brown the
ushed garlic. Remove it and add
e anchovy pieces. Set aside.
lean, boil, and cut the escarole
to strips. Put the oil and an-

chovies back on the heat and add
the escarole, capers, and olives
and cook briefly. Fill the calzone
with this mixture and cook according to the master recipe 124. The
finished calzone should be puffed
up and golden brown.

132
SCHIACCIATINE, No. 1

This is a pita-like bread and is made with the same bread dough as for pizza. For 6 servings you will need:

3½ cups flour, approximately
1 cube (⅔ ounce) compressed yeast dissolved in ½ cup warm water
1 cup water
Pinch of salt
Rosemary leaves
Olive oil

Add water and salt to the yeast mixture, and add flour until the dough becoms too stiff to stir. Turn out onto a floured board and knead in enough flour to form an elastic dough. Let it rest in a cool place (not cold) for half an hour, covered with a towel. Then divide the dough into six portions and roll it out into circles about 4 inches wide and very thin. Moisten each one with a little oil and cook in a preheated 400° oven as with pizza. When the schiacciatine turn golden and are just barely cooked, brush them with a little more oil and sprinkle them with salt and a few rosemary leaves and put them back in the oven for a few more minutes.

Instead of rosemary you can substitute oregano or other herbs.

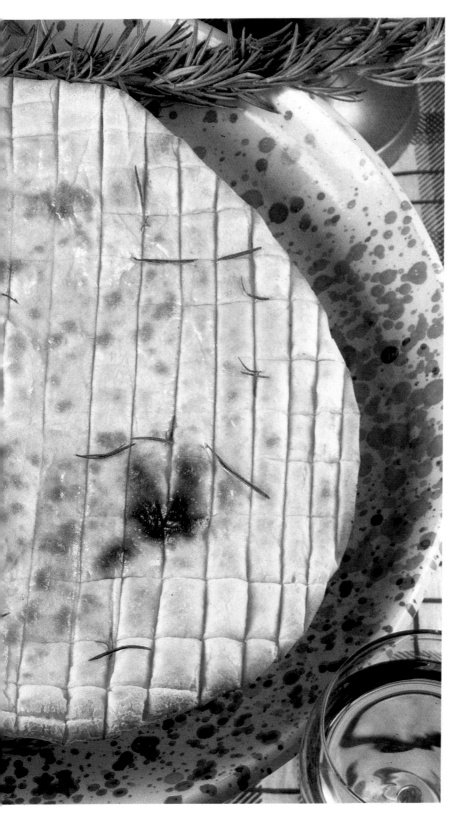

133
SCHIACCIATINE, No. 2

This recipe is similar to the first version, but let the dough rise a little longer this time. Put the circles in the oven without moistening them with any oil and the dough will inflate even more. These *schiacciatine* serve as a good accompaniment to salamis and other antipasto as a kind of hot, light, flavorful bread.

Schiacciatine, No. 1

Part Two

Focaccia, rustic pies and fritters

1
FRITTERS (FRITELLE) WITH SQUASH BLOSSOMS

You will need:

4½ cups flour
1½ cubes (⅔ ounce) compressed yeast
    dissolved in ½ cup of warm water
6–8 cups squash blossoms (10 ounces)
Salt and pepper
Olive oil

Pour the flour into a bowl and add a little salt. Stir in the yeast, dissolved in water, to the flour little by little. Add 2½–3 cups more water until you have a thick batter. Let this rest for an hour, covered with a cloth.

Meanwhile, prepare the squash blossoms. Clean them first, then cut them into strips. When the batter has rested, it will have risen just slightly while remaining fluid.

Add the squash blossoms to it. Add salt and pepper.

Now heat an inch or two of olive oil in a pan. When it is very hot, drop the batter in by spoonfuls to form the frittelle, which will puff up and become golden brown, delicious, and delicate.

Fritters with Mozzarella or Scamorza

2
FRITTERS WITH MOZZARELLA OR SCAMORZA

Follow the master recipe for the batter. Instead of squash blossoms, mix 1½ cups of Mozzarella or Scamorza or any soft cheese, cut in tiny pieces, into the batter.

3
FRITTERS WITH ANCHOVIES

The recipe is identical to the master recipe except that in place of squash blossoms you add tiny pieces of anchovies (about ½ cup) to the batter, washed well to desalt them before cutting them up.

4
FRITTERS WITH SMOKED SALMON

In this version add bits of smoked salmon (about 1 cup) to the batter.

5
FRITTERS WITH SMOKED HERRING

Follow the master recipe for batter and add 1 cup of chopped smoked herring to the batter instead of squash blossoms.

Fritters with Anchovies

6
FRITTERS WITH SMOKED EELS

This time add pieces of smoked eel (about 1 cup) to the batter.

7
FRITTERS WITH CICINIELLI

Cicinielli are the tiny fish found around Naples. Instead of *cicinielli* you can use other tiny fish or fish eggs, which go by various names in Italy: *ceche* (which means blind eels' eggs) in Tuscany, *bianchetti*, *gianchetti*, and *roscetti* in Liguria. Add ½–1 cup to the batter. See recipe 66 in Part One.

8
FRITTERS WITH ANCHOVIES OR OTHER SMOKED OR SALTED FISH AND MOZZARELLA

Mix both bits of fish and Mozzarella cut into cubes (about 1¼ cups in all) into the batter.

9
FRITTERS WITH TOMATOES AND OTHER VEGETABLES

Follow the master recipe for the batter. Add seeded and chopped tomatoes, mixed with chopped celery or strips of zucchini. You will need about 1½ cups of vegetables.

10
FRITTERS WITH TOMATOES, ANCHOVIES, AND MOZZARELLA

Add chopped tomatoes, pieces of anchovy, and cubes of Mozzarella, all cut into tiny pieces and mixed, about 1½ cups altogether, to the batter. Prepare according to the master recipe and they will puff up and become golden.

11
FRIED GNOCCO, REGGIO STYLE

This is simply dough which is enriched and fried. For 6 servings, you will need:

3½ cups flour
1 cube (⅔ ounce) compressed yeast
   dissolved in ½ cup warm water
1 cup lard, softened
Salt
Lard for frying

Make a dough by mixing the flour, the yeast dissolved in the water, the softened lard, and a pinch of salt. Knead well. Add a little more water if necessary to get a soft, smooth, consistent dough. Let this rest for an hour under a cloth. It will rise a little.

Roll it out to a thickness of ¹⁄₁₆ inch and cut it into diamond shapes. Fry these diamonds in a pan with a good amount of very hot lard, then drain them well on absorbent paper.

They are delicious as is, as an accompaniment to salami, ham, or cheese, or with endive or radishes sautéed in a little butter with a slice or two of garlic.

Fried Gnocco, Reggio Style

12
FRIED GNOCCO, MODENA STYLE

This recipe is the same as the one above but calls for chopped fatback instead of lard in the dough.

13
CRESCENTINE

These are almost the same as the fried gnocco, but they are called *crescentine* in Bologna and are a bit thicker and cut in circles instead of diamonds. You can add bits of chopped ham or prosciutto to the dough.

14
CHISOLINI

These are part of the *gnocco* and the *crescentine* family, and come from Mantua. For 6 servings you will need:

3½ cups flour
Salt
1 cube (⅔ ounce) compressed yeast dissolved in ½ cup warm water
2 ounces butter, at room temperature
2 tablespoons milk
Olive oil or shortening

Make a dough combining the flour, a pinch of salt, and the yeast dissolved in water. Let this rest a little, then work in the butter, and finally the milk, adding more water if necessary, to get a rather soft but consistent dough.

Pull off small pieces of the dough and flatten them into diamond-shaped pieces about 1/16 inch thick. Fry them in an abundant amount of very hot olive oil or shortening. They should puff up a little during cooking. Turn them over as they cook so that both sides turn a golden brown. Eat these as an accompaniment to cheese, ham, or salami.

15
BURT-LENA

This is the Piacenza version of fried dough and it is still made this way in the area going toward the Apennines. The dough and the cooking are the same as for fried *gnocco* (recipe 12), but add less flour so that the dough is a bit softer, like a *frittelle*.

16
FRIED PIZZA, No. 1

These are circles of dough on which a filling is spread on one half and the other side is folded over it, like a small calzone. The main difference between them is that the calzone is baked and these little

pizzas are fried. For 6 servings, you will need:

    3½ cups flour
    1 cup water
    Salt

Work together the flour with the water and a pinch of salt until you have a firm dough. (The yeast is omitted in this recipe.) Let it rest for about half an hour and then divide it into 6 small balls and roll each one out to a thickness of 1/16 inch and 4½–6 inches in diameter.

The filling can be made in various ways. The best known perhaps, and also the easiest, is a slice of Mozzarella and a few pieces

of anchovy. Ten ounces of Mozzarella and 4 or 5 anchovies, washed well to get rid of the salt, should be enough for 6. Fold the edge over the stuffing, pinch the edges together to form a tight seal, and fry gently in plenty of hot oil.

17
FRIED PIZZA, No. 2

The recipe is the same as above, but add a tablespoon of crushed tomatoes to each pizza before sealing and frying as above.

Crescentine (left)

Fried Pizza, No. 1 (right)

18
FRIED PIZZA, No. 3

This is also a classic version. For the filling mix 3 or 4 eggs with 8 ounces of Ricotta, 2–3 tablespoons of peeled and cubed fresh sausage, and ¼ cup chopped parsley.

19
FRIED PIZZA, No. 4

Instead of the raw eggs of variation number 3, use boiled eggs and chopped black olives.

20
FRIED PIZZA, No. 5

These are more elementary than the others, but still delicious. The dough is the same as described above but you make circles 3–4 inches in diameter and ¹⁄₁₆ inch thick. Fry them in plenty of hot oil,

then drain them and immediately garnish them with tomato sauce and fresh basil leaves. The heat of the pizza will heat the tomatoes, and they are eaten as is.

Of course they can also be garnished with Mozzarella or other ingredients, but there is not the same affinity as with the tomatoes, which need nothing more than the

Sgabei—Donzelline

heat of the pizza and the basil to liven them up.

21
SGABEI— DONZELLINE

These are made with leavened dough and no other ingredients are added to the dough. Make a dough following the recipe for fritters (recipe 1 of this section), but use only enough water to form a soft dough. Let the dough rest for half an hour in a warm place covered with a cloth. Then, on a pastry board, divide it into pieces and roll out each piece into the shape of a finger about 4 inches long and ½ inch wide, more or less. Fry these *sgabei* in ½ inch of hot oil. They will swell a little as they fry, like thick homemade breadsticks. They are extremely tasty, with a rustic simplicity, and are ideal as an accompaniment to ham and cheese. The *sgabei* still have a place of honor in Lunigiana.

In some parts of Tuscany, little pieces of fried bread dough, similar to the *sgabei* but smaller, are charming called *donzelline*, meaning "little ladies." Sometimes a sprinkling of chopped thyme or other herbs is added to the dough.

22
SCIATT

Sciatt, which means "toad," is a fritter of dough enriched with cheese, as made in Valtellina, a mountainous region in northern Italy. The dough can be made with buckwheat flour and white flour in equal parts, or two-thirds of the buckwheat and one-third of the white. Altogether you will need 3½ cups of flour.

Mix the flour and a pinch of salt together and add about 2 cups of water to get a thick batter. Let this rest for an hour, then add a bland cheese such as Mozzarella, cut into pieces, and a small glass of grappa or brandy. Mix this well so that the cheese is evenly distributed throughout the batter, then drop it by spoonfuls in an iron skillet in which you've heated ½ inch of olive oil. Let them become golden brown on both sides so the cheese melts. (Be sure you have included some cheese in each spoonful before you drop it into the skillet.) Drain them well on absorbent paper and serve hot.

23
PANZEROTTI, No. 1

These are small fried pizzas made with a dough that is lighter than the usual pizza dough. For 6 servings you will need:

3½ cups flour
1 cube (⅔ ounce) compressed yeast dissolved in ½ cup warm water

Add a pinch of salt to the flour and then little by little the yeast dissolved in water. Add more water if you see the dough is becoming too dry. Let it rest for half an hour in a cool spot, then divide it into 6 small pieces. Knead well. Roll out each one into a circle about ¹⁄₁₆ inch thick. On one half of the circle, put a few slices of Mozzarella (10 ounces total for the 6 *panzerotti*), and one or two pieces of anchovy, washed first to remove the saltiness. Then fold the other side over it, pinch the edges together gently, and fry in oil.

You could also add a little crushed tomato to the filling instead of the anchovies or use all three — tomatoes, cheese, and anchovies — always a pleasing combination in these little pizzas.

24
PANZEROTTI, No. 2

Follow the recipe in the first version, but make the filling as follows: Mix 3 or 4 eggs with 2 tablespoons of Ricotta and 3 tablespoons of cooked sausage. Spread over the pizza and continue as above.

25
CHIZZE

These are a kind of *panzerotti* with roots in the Emilia region. For 6 servings you will need:

> 3½ cups flour
> 1 cube (⅔ ounce) compressed yeast dissolved in ½ cup tepid water
> 4 tablespoons lard
> Salt
> Grated Parmesan cheese
> Olive oil

Mix the flour with the yeast dissolved in water. Work in the lard and add a pinch of salt. The dough should be smooth and firm. Add more water little by little until it is the proper consistency. Let this rest for half an hour in a cool spot, covered with a cloth. Then roll it out to a thickness of ¹⁄₁₆ inch and cut it into squares approximately 4 inches to a side. Cover half of each square with a tablespoon of Parmesan or some other

Panzerotti, No. 1

softer cheese. Fold the other side over it, pinch the edges together to form a seal, and fry these *chizze* in a skillet in ½ inch of oil. Drain them well on absorbent paper and serve immediately.

26
CASSONI, No. 1

These are another type of *panzerotti*, Emilia style. For 6 servings you will need:

> 3½ cups flour
> 3 eggs
> 3 tablespoons milk (more if needed)
> Salt
> 2 pounds spinach, beet greens, or other greens
> 3–4 tablespoons grated Parmesan cheese

Make a dough with the flour, eggs, and milk, adding a pinch of salt, so that you get a smooth but firm dough. Roll the dough out and cut circles 4–5 inches in diameter. On one half of each circle spread a little of a filling made like this:

Clean and boil 2 pounds of spinach, beet greens, or other greens in a very little water. Drain them well and cut them up very finely. Mix 3–4 tablespoons of grated cheese with them and divide this among the circles. Fold the free side over the filling and pinch the edges together firmly. Fry in ½ inch of lard, drain on absorbent paper, and serve hot.

In another version, a filling is made with onions cooked gently in butter.

27
CASSONI, No. 2

In the old-fashioned version, the filling is made with a mixture of greens, boiled and chopped as in the preceding recipe; then raisins, first revived in warm water and then drained, and chopped pine nuts are added. Otherwise the recipe is the same as the preceding one.

28
CALCIONI ABRUZZESI

This is a stuffed and fried dough. For 6 servings you will need:

   3½ cups flour
   2 eggs

Cassoni, No. 1 (left)
Calcioni Abruzzesi (right)

¼ cup lard

Salt

1–2 tablespoons lemon juice, to taste

Mix the flour, eggs, lard, a pinch of salt, and lemon juice together with enough water to obtain a soft but firm dough. Let this rest for a while and in the meantime prepare the filling. You will need:

1¼ cups Ricotta cheese

2 egg yolks

¾ cup ham, cut into cubes

¾ cup Provolone cheese, cut into cubes

¼ cup chopped parsley

Salt and pepper

Combine these ingredients, adding salt and pepper to taste. Now roll out the dough into 2 thin sheets. On one of the sheets, distribute the filling at regular intervals. Then cover with the second sheet. Press the unfilled space around the fillings together and then cut around them with a small cutting wheel.

Fry these *calcioni* in a generous amount of hot oil, then drain them well on absorbent paper before serving. In the Abruzzo they almost

always eat vegetables, pieces of Scamorza cheese, and brains fried to form what is called a *fritto misto*, as an accompaniment to the *calcioni*.

29
PANZEROTTI, ROMAN STYLE, No. 1

There is an important variation in the dough for *Panzerotti, Roman Style*. For 6 servings you will need:

2½ cups flour
Salt
3 egg yolks
4 tablespoons butter, softened

Add a pinch of salt to the flour and mix it with the egg yolks and butter. Add enough water to make a soft, elastic dough. Roll this dough out into a sheet, not too thin, and make circles 4½–6 inches in diameter. On one half of each circle, spread a filling made with:

¾ cup ham, cut into small cubes
¾ cup cheese like Gruyère or Fontina, cut into small cubes
2 eggs
2 tablespoons Parmesan cheese
Salt and pepper

Combine these ingredients to make a soft, but not too dry, mixture. Spread this filling on the circles and fold the edges over,

pressing them together to form a seal. You can also use the leftover egg whites to paste the edges together.

Fry these Roman-style *panzerotti* in a pan with plenty of hot oil, turning as they cook.

30
PANZEROTTI, ROMAN STYLE, No. 2

The dough is the same as described above, but the filling is lighter. You will need:

1 medium onion, chopped
4 tablespoons olive oil
6 anchovy fillets, cut into pieces
1½ cups Mozzarella cheese, cut in small cubes

Sauté the onion in the oil with the anchovies. Remove from heat and add the cheese, stirring well to blend the flavors. Fill the *panzerotti* as in the preceding recipe and continue as above.

31
TIGELLE, No. 1

This is a dish that no doubt dates back a long way, from the days when man began to mix flour and water and roast it simply, over red-hot stones. *Tigelle* are still made like this in the Apennines today, though in a slightly less crude way. For 6 servings you will need:

3½ cups flour
Salt

1 cube (⅔ ounce) compressed yeast dissolved in ½ cup warm water
2 ounces lard
½ cup chopped fatback
Garlic
Rosemary

Add a pinch of salt to the flour, then work in the yeast and the lard and enough water to get a smooth, well-mixed dough. Let this rise in a warm place for an hour, covered with a cloth, then roll out a sheet 1/16 inch thick. Cut circles about 4 inches in diameter and fry them in hot lard to cover. Drain them well, then slice them across, horizontally, to form 2 circles. On one half, spread a seasoning made of ground or chopped fatback — about 2 ounces — garlic to taste, and a few rosemary leaves. Cover with the top and serve hot.

In the traditional method, no yeast is added and the dough is tougher and heavier. To be completely authentic the circles are baked on clay disks, greased with lard, called *tigelli*, that were made just for this purpose and are still found in that area. The circles of dough on the *tigelli* are put on the open hearth to bake, over the coals, thus absorbing the aroma of the chestnut leaves that are placed between them. Today, of course, a gas or electric stove has mostly replaced the *tigelli* and hearth method.

Tigelle, No. 1

32
TIGELLE, No. 2

These *tigelle* are prepared the same as in the first version, but the filling consists of fresh grated Pecorino or Romano cheese, which the heat of the *tigelle* should melt nicely.

33
PIADINA

Like the *tigelle*, the *piadina* are part of the most ancient heritage of breadmaking. They come from the Po River area in the Romagna region, while the *tigelle* come from the mountains. For 6 servings you will need:

> 4½ cups flour
> Salt
> ¾ cup lard, softened
> ½ cup water, approximately

Add a pinch of salt to the flour and work in the lard, adding enough tepid water to get a soft but consistent dough. Divide this dough into pieces and shape them into circles about 1⁄16 inch thick. These *piadine* are cooked, with no other oil or additives, in an iron skillet. They were originally cooked on large clay disks called *testi*, or on cast iron, which is still used by some people today. A trick to make them softer is to prick the rounds with a fork as they cook. The *piadine* are still used as bread in Romagna. They can also be covered or filled with ham or cheese.

Another very appetizing version is to cut them in half, fill them with watercress and cheese, and serve as sandwiches, hot or cold.

34
CROSTATA WITH ONIONS, RUSTIC STYLE

The rustic-style *crostata* is a pie that differs from the rustic-style tart in that the dough is more delicate and the preparation is more elaborate. While bread dough is often used for the *focaccia* and the rustic tart, for the *crostata* you must use the following dough. For 6 servings you will need:

> 2½ cups flour
> Salt
> ¾ cup butter, softened
> ¼ cup cold water, approximately

Add a pinch of salt to the flour and work the flour and butter together, mixing them so the butter is as well absorbed as possible. Continue to work it together and add water little by little as needed to get a homogenous, smooth and elastic dough, but do this more gently than with previous doughs. Finally shape it into a ball and let it rest for half an hour in a cool place, covered with a cloth.

Meanwhile prepare a filling. You will need:

> 6–8 medium onions, chopped
> 4 tablespoons butter
> 6 anchovies, washed and chopped
> 1 tablespoon flour
> ½ cup cream
> Salt and pepper
> 1 egg, beaten

Cook the onions in the butter until they are translucent, along

Crostata with Onions, Rustic Style

with the anchovies. When the onions are ready and the anchovy has begun to melt, add the flour and the cream, stirring well so that it thickens. Add salt and pepper to taste. Remove from the fire and quickly mix in the beaten egg.

When the dough has rested sufficiently, work it again briefly, then roll it out into a round sheet about 1/16 inch thick. Butter a round pizza pan and flour it and put the sheet of dough on it, pushing up the edges to form a low ridge. Prick the surface of the dough with a fork.

Pour the filling mixture over the dough and bake in a preheated 400° oven until the filling has set and the crust is golden. Cut into pieces to serve.

If you have any leftover dough, you can make a latticework to cover the filling. Another touch is to boil separately 12 baby onions, sauté them in a little butter, and place them around the edge of the sheet before putting it in the oven.

Another method is to bake the dough separately for 20 minutes, weighing the surface down with dried beans. The sheet of dough will be rather dry with this method. Remove the beans, spread the filling over the dough, and put it

back in the oven for about 10 more minutes.

35
CROSTATA WITH LEEKS

The recipe is similar but the filling is a little different. For 6 servings you will need:

Dough, as prepared in the master recipe 34

10–12 leeks

2 tablespoons oil

2 tablespoons butter

3 eggs, beaten

½ cup cream

3 tablespoons grated Parmesan cheese

Clean the leeks well and cut the white part into slices. Melt the butter in the oil over a low flame and add the leeks, cooking them gently so they do not brown. Remove from heat and add salt and pepper, the eggs, cream, and cheese. Mix well and pour over the dough and bake as in recipe 34.

36
CROSTATA WITH GREEN PEPPERS

For 6 servings you will need:

Dough, as prepared in the master recipe 34

4–5 green peppers, cleaned, seeded and cut in strips

6 tablespoons oil

4 tomatoes, peeled and seeded (see page 23) and cut in pieces

1 large onion, sliced

The peppers can also be roasted under a grill or over a flame and then peeled. Heat the oil in a pan and add the other ingredients. Let them cook over moderate heat, stirring occasionally, until they have become soft. Drain off excess oil, then pour the mixture over the sheet of dough and continue as in recipe 34.

37
CROSTATA WITH CARROTS

For 6 servings you will need:

Dough, as prepared in the master recipe 34
10–12 carrots (1 pound), peeled, boiled and sliced
4 tablespoons butter
¼ cup beef or chicken broth
Salt and pepper
4 ounces Mozzarella cheese, in thin slices
2 tablespoons grated Parmesan cheese
Butter

Sauté the boiled carrots in the butter, adding a little broth as necessary to keep the bottom of the pan liquid. Let this thicken a little and add salt and pepper. Set aside a small amount and force the rest through a sieve or put in the blender. Pour the puree over the dough, rolled out in the baking pan. Place the slices of Mozzarella over the carrots, then garnish with the carrots that were set aside. Sprinkle the Parmesan over this, dot with butter, and continue as in recipe 34.

Crostata with Leeks (left)

Crostata with Green Peppers (right)

38
CROSTATA WITH ZUCCHINI

For 6 servings you will need:

Dough, as prepared in the master recipe 34
2 tablespoons oil
2 tablespoons butter
1 large onion, chopped
4–6 small zucchini, sliced

2 tomatoes, peeled and seeded (see page 23) and crushed (optional)
Salt and pepper
2 eggs, beaten
2 tablespoons grated Parmesan cheese

Make a *soffritto* by sautéing the onion in the butter and oil, then add the zucchini. Sauté briefly, then add the tomatoes, salt, and pepper. When they are cooked,

Crostata with Carrots

remove from the heat and immediately add the eggs and cheese. Pour the filling over the rolled dough and continue as in recipe 34.

39
CROSTATA WITH GREENS

For 6 servings, you will need:

Dough, as prepared in the master recipe 34

6 cups spinach, beet greens, or other greens, boiled, drained, and chopped

2 tablespoons butter

2 tablespoons oil

1 tablespoon flour

½ cup hot milk

Salt and pepper

2–3 eggs, beaten

3 tablespoons Parmesan cheese, grated

Sauté the greens in the oil and butter 2–3 minutes. Add the flour, cook for a few minutes to thicken it, and then add the milk, salt and pepper. Remove from heat and add the eggs and cheese to get a rather thick mixture. Spread this over the dough and continue as in recipe 34.

A variation is to add 4–6 ounces of Ricotta to the spinach and ¼ cup raisins, revived in a little warm water and drained, and ¼ cup chopped pine nuts. In this case you can omit the eggs and Parmesan cheese.

40
CROSTATA WITH ARTICHOKES AND CHEESE

For 6 servings you will need:

Dough, as prepared in the master recipe 34

12 artichoke hearts, cleaned and cut into slices (or use frozen or canned, well-drained)

1 tablespoon lemon juice (optional, see directions)

4 tablespoons butter

Salt and pepper

¼ cup chopped parsley

1 cup Fontina, Gruyère or Taleggio cheese or a mixture, cubed

3 tablespoons Parmesan cheese

¾ cup cream

Crostata with Zucchini

Put the artichokes in water with 1 tablespoon lemon juice until you are ready to use them, to avoid discoloration. Dry them, then brown them in the butter, adding salt, pepper, and the parsley. Spread them over the dough and cover with the cheese. Finally sprinkle the Parmesan over this, then the cream, and bake as in recipe 34.

41
MOZZARELLA IN CARROZZA

This is a very delicious combination of bread and Mozzarella. It should be eaten as soon as it is prepared, while it is still hot. Unfortunately it is often made ahead in pizzerias and allowed to cool, and this diminishes its appeal. For 6 servings you will need:

24 slices of Italian white bread, about ⅜ inch thick
12 slices of Mozzarella, about ¾ inch thick (twice as thick as the bread and the same size)
3 or more beaten eggs
Flour
3 tablespoons milk (more if necessary)
Pepper
Olive oil

Put each slice of cheese between 2 slices of bread. Dredge the sandwich in the flour, then immerse it in the egg mixed with the milk. Let the sandwiches soak in this liquid for half an hour, turning them once or twice. Then heat ¼

Mozzarella in Carrozza

inch of olive oil in a frying pan and fry the sandwiches until they are golden brown on both sides. Drain them well and serve immediately. Just before serving you can grind a little fresh pepper over them.

42
CROSTATA WITH MUSHROOMS, No. 1

The dough for this crostata is the same as in recipe 34. For the filling you will need:

> 2 cups fresh mushrooms, sliced
> ½ cup butter
> Salt and pepper
> ½ cup dry white wine or Marsala
> 3 ounces cream

Sauté the mushrooms lightly in the butter. Add salt, pepper, and the wine, and continue to cook for a moment. Then add the cream, stir to blend, and remove from the heat. Pour this over the dough and continue as in the recipe 34. For variation, you can add béchamel sauce instead of cream.

43
CROSTATA WITH MUSHROOMS, No. 2

For this version, prepare the mushrooms as in the preceding recipe, remove them from the heat, let them cool, and add the following mixture to them. You will need:

1¼ cups Ricotta cheese
3 eggs, separated
3 tablespoons Parmesan cheese

Mix the Ricotta with the egg yolks and Parmesan and add salt and pepper to taste. Blend this in with the mushrooms. Beat the whites until they are stiff and then gently fold them into the mushroom-cheese mixture. Pour this over the dough and bake as in recipe 34.

In a still richer version, you can add ¾ cup of diced ham to the mushrooms.

44
CROSTATA WITH CHEESE

For this recipe from the Valdaosta region you will need:

Dough, as prepared in the master recipe 34
10 ounces Fontina cheese or others such as Gruyère or Taleggio
3 eggs, beaten
3 tablespoons grated Parmesan cheese
½ cup white wine
Nutmeg
Salt and pepper

Cut the Fontina into thin strips and cover the dough with them. Mix the eggs with the Parmesan and the wine, adding a dash of nutmeg and salt and pepper to taste. Pour this over the dough and continue as in recipe 34.

45
CROSTATA WITH HAM, No. 1

You will need:

Dough, as prepared in the master recipe 34
4 eggs, beaten
¾ cup cream
Nutmeg
Salt and pepper
2 cups ham, diced

Beat the eggs with the cream, add a dash of nutmeg, salt and pepper to taste, and the diced ham. Pour this over the *crostata* dough and continue as in recipe 34.

46
CROSTATA WITH HAM, No. 2

You will need:

Dough, as prepared in the master recipe 34
4 eggs, beaten
½ cup cream
Nutmeg
Salt and pepper
1½ cups diced ham
1½ cups diced Mozzarella cheese

Beat the eggs with the cream, and add a dash of nutmeg, salt and pepper. Sprinkle the ham and cheese over the dough and pour the egg mixture on top. Continue as in recipe 34.

47
CROSTATA WITH PANCETTA

This recipe calls for *pancetta*, which is a kind of rolled, very fatty ham (see recipe 102 in Part One). You can substitute bacon for *pancetta*. For this recipe you will need:

Dough, as prepared in the master recipe 34
3 eggs
½ cup cream
8 ounces *pancetta* or bacon, cut into very thin slices
8 ounces Gruyère or Fontina cheese, cut into thin slices

Beat the eggs with the cream, adding salt and pepper to taste. Spread alternating layers of cheese and *pancetta* over the dough and cover with the egg-cream mixture. Proceed as in recipe 34.

48
CROSTATA WITH RICOTTA AND SAUSAGE

You will need:

Dough, as prepared in the master recipe 34

Crostata with Mushrooms, No. 1

1¼ cups Ricotta

3 egg yolks

1 cup sausage, crumbled or cut into cubes

3 tablespoons Parmesan cheese, grated

Salt and pepper

Nutmeg

Mix the Ricotta with the egg yolks, the sausage, and the Parmesan. Season with salt and pepper and a dash of nutmeg. Blend this together and pour it into the dough. Continue as in recipe 34.

49
BORLENGHI

This recipe is also one of the oldest dishes coming from the Emilian region between Modena and its border with Tuscany. To make this you will need:

2¾ cups flour

2 cups water, approximately

Salt

Lard

¼ pound fatback

6 cloves garlic

1 teaspoon rosemary

Make a batter by adding water to the flour little by little until it is fluid and not too thick. Add a pinch of salt. Heat the biggest iron skillet you can find. Grease it lightly with lard and pour in a big spoonful of the batter so that it covers the bottom of the pan, forming a very thin pancake, which is almost a lacework, and cooks in an instant. As they cook, spread a tablespoon of seasoning made by mashing together the fatback, garlic, and rosemary. Cook the *borlenghi* one

Crostata with Ricotta and Sausage

by one, and drain on absorbent paper. They are best served very hot.

50
TESTAROI—PANICACCI

At the top of the hills of Lerici, surrounding a castle built before A.D. 1000, is the little region of Trebiano, still intact with its medieval houses and narrow streets. At the foot of the castle is the Locanda delle Sette Lune, a trattoria where Lucia makes old-fashioned dishes like *testaroi* or *testaroli*, a name which comes from the Latin word *testum*, meaning "earthen pot." These *testaroi* are another in this group of fried or cooked dough, and in fact it is one of the oldest doughs in the world. It goes back to the time when *schiacciata*, bread, and pizza were all the same, just used in different ways.

Lucia makes her dough with spelt flour, which is a grain from the ancient world that is still collected in this region of Lunigiana, although each year there is less. For our purposes, regular wheat flour, water, and salt are used, nothing else.

For 6 servings, you will need 4½ cups of flour. Mix this with salt and about 4 cups water to make a somewhat thin batter. Now heat a pan, preferably cast iron, which can substitute for the old-fashioned

earthenware pots that were used. Do not grease this at all (although one trick to avoid sticking is to wipe it with a potato cut in half and greased with a little oil). When the pan is hot, pour a little batter over it, dripping it to form a circle that will cook quickly without sticking, lightly roasting.

The *testaroi* are seasoned with the classic Ligurian pesto, made with basil, oil, Pecorino and *prescinseua*, a kind of farmer's cheese, pounded or chopped in a food processor, along with a few pine nuts. Or it is simply seasoned

with oil and grated Pecorino. I would consider them a kind of *schiacciata* or *pizzetta*. They are quite separate from those *testaroi* which are larger and cut into strips and thrown into a pot of vegetables just like the ancient Roman *laganum*, the ancestor of *tagliatelle*.

The *testaroi* are made smaller in other versions and the batter is thicker. The cooking is done on smaller earthenware disks and they are then called *panicacci*.

Testaroi—Panicacci

51
FOCACCIA

Focaccia is rather like a very thick pizza with a more breadlike texture. It is usually seasoned lightly and eaten as a snack. You will need:

4½ cups flour
Salt
1½ cubes (⅔ ounce) compressed yeast dissolved in ½ cup warm water

Mix a pinch of salt with the flour and add the yeast and about ½ cup of water to make a soft but firm dough. Knead until smooth and elastic. Let this rise at least half an hour, then roll it out and put it in a greased baking pan. It should be about 1½ inches thick. Let this cook in a preheated 400° oven for about 30–45 minutes. Let it cool before cutting and serving. It is very good with cheese, ham, salami, and so on.

You can make a softer and more flavorful *focaccia* by mixing ½ cup of the flour with the yeast and water and letting this rise for half an hour in a warm place covered with a cloth. Then mix in the remaining flour, adding 2–3 tablespoons lard or oil. You can also add a few leaves of rosemary or sage, finely chopped, to the dough as you knead it.

Focaccia

Focaccia with Tomato and Garlic

52
FOCACCIA WITH TOMATO AND GARLIC

This version of *focaccia* is characteristic of Puglia in southern Italy where it is called *puddica*. The dough is the same as that described above in the simpler version. Roll it out in the *focaccia* shape in a baking pan greased with oil and then poke little indentations on the surface with your finger and put little pieces of garlic and tomatoes in them. Sprinkle with salt and oregano, moisten with oil, and bake in a preheated 400° oven for 30–40 minutes.

53
PIZZA RUSTICA, No. 1

Although this is called a pizza, it is actually a *focaccia*. For the dough you will need:

3½ cups flour
Salt
4 tablespoons olive oil
¾ cup water or white wine, approximately

Add a pinch of salt to the flour and combine the oil and flour, then add water or white wine (the old-fashiond Puglian way) little by little until you get a soft dough. Knead until smooth and elastic. There is no yeast. Now prepare this filling. You will need:

1 cup Ricotta cheese
1½ cup Mozzarella cheese, in cubes
1 cup soft cheese, like Bel Paese, cubed
1 cup sausage, preferably a spicy one, cubed
3 or 4 eggs, beaten

Mix the Ricotta, the Mozzarella, the soft cheese, the sausage, and the eggs. Set aside. Roll the dough out into 2 sheets about ¹⁄₁₆ inch thick, with one a little larger than the other. They should fit into a round greased baking pan and the larger sheet, which will go on the bottom, should be big enough to go up the sides a little so as to form a rim. Spread the filling on it, then cover with the second sheet and pinch the edges together. Brush with a little beaten egg and put in a preheated 400° oven for 45 minutes.

As an alternative, you can cover the top with a latticework made from the dough, instead of the second sheet.

54
PIZZA RUSTICA, No. 2

Replace the sausage with ham, which you can first sauté briefly in a little olive oil. The other ingredients are the same.

55
FOCACCIA WITH ONIONS, UMBRIAN STYLE

For 6 servings you will need:

3 cups flour
1½ cubes (⅔ ounce) compressed yeast dissolved in ½ cup water
⅓ cup lard, softened
4 tablespoons oil
Salt
3 medium onions, thinly sliced
Fresh sage, minced

Make a starter dough with ½ cup flour and the yeast dissolved in water. Let this rise in a warm place, covered with a cloth, for an hour. Then work in the rest of the flour, again adding water, little by little as needed. Knead until smooth and elastic. Shape the dough into a ball, cut an incision on top in the shape of a cross, and put it in a warm place to rise, covered with a cloth, for 2 hours. When the dough has risen, knead it a third time, kneading in the lard, the oil, and a pinch of salt. Grease a round pan and spread the dough over the bottom. Scatter the sliced onions over the dough, sprinkle a handful of fresh sage over the *focaccia*, moisten with oil, and let this rise at least half an hour. Then put it in a preheated 400° oven and bake until it is golden brown.

Focaccia with Onions, Umbrian Style

56
FOCACCIA WITH ONIONS, LIGURIAN STYLE

There was a time when this was sold in railway stations, especially early in the morning, to the travelers arriving after an uncomfortable night on the train. The recipe for this *focaccia* was given to me by my friends Gianna and Vittorio Bisso and Gianni Carbone, in Recco. For 6 servings you will need:

3½ cups flour
1 cube (⅔ ounce) compressed yeast dissolved in ½ cup warm water
Salt
Olive oil
½ cup onions, sliced

Work the yeast dissolved in water into the flour, adding a pinch of salt and enough water, little by little, to make a soft but firm dough. Knead well. Let it rise in a cool spot for half an hour, covered with a cloth. When you are ready to use it, roll it out to a thickness of 1½ inches and place on a greased round baking sheet. Poke little indentations on the surface with your finger and dribble a light flavorful olive oil over this, then strew ½ cup of onions over the top, sprinkle with salt, and bake until golden brown in a preheated 400° oven.

57
SFINCIUNI

A rustic dish from the Palermo kitchen that is a bit complicated but enchanting. For 6 servings you will need:

⅓ cup olive oil
Juice of 1 lemon
Salt and pepper
4 tablespoons Pecorino, Romano, or Caciocavallo cheese, grated
3½ cups flour
1½ cubes (⅔ ounce) compressed yeast dissolved in ½ cup water

Warm the olive oil and add the lemon juice, salt, pepper, and cheese. Work this mixture into the flour, then add the yeast. You should get a soft but firm dough.

Focaccia with Onions, Ligurian Style

Knead well. Put it into a bowl dusted with a little flour, make a cross-shaped incision in the top, and let it rest for 2 hours, covered with a cloth, in a warm place.

For the topping you will need:

⅓ cup olive oil
1 large onion, chopped
3 or 4 tomatoes, peeled and seeded (see page 23), chopped

¼ cup chopped parsley
¾ cup Pecorino, Romano, or Caciocavallo cheese, cut into small pieces
4 anchovy fillets, washed and cut into pieces
4 tablespoons olive oil
2 tablespoons dry breadcrumbs
Anchovies for garnish

While the dough rises, prepare the topping. Heat the oil in a pan

and add the onion and the to-matoes. Let them cook for a few minutes, then add the parsley, the cheese, and the anchovies. Let this cook gently over a low flame for 10–15 minutes. Then set aside.

When the 2 hours have passed, briefly knead the dough again and spread it on a greased round baking pan. Let it rise for another half-hour in a warm place. When the dough is ready, poke indentations into the top with your finger and spread half the sauce over it. Bake in a preheated 400° oven for half an hour.

In the meantime, heat 4 more tablespoons of oil in a frying pan with 2 tablespoons of dry bread-crumbs. Take the *focaccia* or *sfinciuni* out of the oven and cover it with the rest of the sauce, garnish it with a few more pieces of chopped anchovy, and cover it all with the breadcrumbs. Moisten with a little fresh oil and put it back in the oven for another 10 minutes to bind it all together, and serve.

58
FOCACCIA (GNOCCO) WITH CICCIOLI, No. 1

Ciccioli are the solid parts that remain after you melt the fat from pork to get lard. A possible sub-stitution might be finely crumbled

Focaccia (Gnocco) with Ciccioli, No. 1

cooked bacon. For 6 servings you will need:

    5 cups flour
    1½ cubes (⅔ ounce) compressed yeast
        dissolved in 1 cup warm water
    ¾ cup lard, softened
    2 cups *ciccioli* or finely crumbled
        cooked bacon

Work the flour, yeast dissolved in water, and lard together on a pastry board. Reserve ½ cup of the *ciccioli* or bacon, adding the rest to the dough. Knead it until it is very smooth and soft and the *ciccioli* are well distributed. Spread the *focac-cia* in a greased baking pan with high sides. Sprinkle the reserved *ciccioli* over the dough, pressing them gently into the dough. Let this rise for about an hour and then bake in a preheated 400° oven. It is ready when it has puffed up and become golden on top. You can enjoy it just out of the oven, but it is equally good cold.

59
FOCACCIA WITH CICCIOLI, No. 2

For this version of *focaccia* with *ciccioli* you will need:

    5 cups flour
    4 eggs, beaten
    1½ cups *ciccioli* or finely crumbled
        cooked bacon

Both lard and yeast are omitted in this recipe. Work the flour into the eggs and continue in the same way as the first version. The recipe

is even better if instead of making one large *focaccia* you make sev-eral that are cooked on one or more baking pans. In the Friuli region in northern Italy this *focaccia* is called *pan de frizze*.

60
FOCACCIA WITH CICCIOLI, No. 3

This is a southern version of *focaccia* and it is called pizza, or sometimes *sfrizzoli*, though it is really a *focaccia*. You will need:

    3½ cups flour
    1 cube (⅔ ounce) compressed yeast
        dissolved in ½ cup warm water
    ½ cup lard
    3 egg yolks
    Grated rind of 1 lemon
    1 cup *ciccioli* or finely crumbled
        cooked bacon

Combine the flour and the yeast dissolved in water. Then work in the lard, the egg yolks, the lemon rind, and the *ciccioli* or bacon. Knead this until you have a smooth, elastic dough. Let it rest in a cool spot, covered with a cloth, for just over an hour. Then roll it out and put it on a greased and floured baking pan and bake in a preheated 400° oven until golden.

61
FOCACCIA WITH CICCIOLI, No. 4

This is the Calabrian version from the Reggio Calabria province and especially from Ardore. For 6 servings you will need:

4½ cups flour
Salt
1½ cubes (⅔ ounce) compressed yeast dissolved in ½ cup warm water
3 tablespoons olive oil
3 eggs, beaten

Add a pinch of salt to the flour and mix it with the yeast dissolved in water, adding more water little by little to get a soft but firm dough. Knead well. Let it rise for an hour, covered with a cloth, in a cool place. Then rework the dough to incorporate the olive oil and eggs, adding more flour if necessary and kneading it until smooth and pliable. Then divide it into two pieces, one slightly larger than the other, and roll them into two sheets about ½ inch thick. Use the larger one to line a greased round baking sheet.

Make a filling by mixing together the following ingredients:

½ cup Ricotta cheese
3 hard-boiled eggs, sliced
1½ cups *ciccioli* or finely crumbled cooked bacon
1 cup ham or prosciutto, diced
4 ounces Mozzarella or Provolone cheese, sliced

Spread this filling over the bottom crust, cover with the top sheet, pinch the edges together, and set it aside to rise for another hour. Then bake in a preheated 400° oven for half an hour until brown. Check from time to time to be sure it isn't browning too fast; if so, cover loosely with a sheet of aluminum foil.

62
TORTANO WITH CICOLI

In Naples *ciccioli* are called *cicoli* and there is a pizza or tart made with them called *tortano*, a very special dish different from the others of its kind. For 6 servings you will need:

4½ cups flour

1 cube (⅔ ounce) compressed yeast dissolved in ½ cup warm water

½ cup lard

1 cup *ciccioli* or finely crumbled cooked bacon

Make a starter dough with ½ cup flour, the yeast dissolved in water, and a good sprinkling of coarsely ground pepper. Let this

Sardenaira, No. 1

rise in a cool place under a cloth for an hour. Then pour the rest of the flour and the salt onto a pastry board, make a well in the center, and put the starter dough there. Gradually work it together, adding the lard and the *ciccioli*. Add a little water if needed to get a smooth dough. Knead this and then let it rise in a cool spot for half an hour. Briefly knead again, spread onto a greased baking pan, and bake in a preheated 400° oven until it is golden.

The classic version of this "pizza" uses a round cooking pan with high sides and a hole in the middle as is used for angel food cakes, which makes the cooking easier.

63 SARDENAIRA, No. 1

Although this is called a Sardenaira pizza, it is really a *focaccia*. In Liguria, where it is from, it is also called a *pizzalandrea*, which is a simplification of "pizza all' Andrea," from the name of the famous admiral, Andrea Doria, who is supposed to have invented it (or more probably, liked it so much that it was dedicated to him). For 6 servings you will need:

4½ cup flour

1½ cubes (⅔ ounce) compressed yeast dissolved in ½ cup warm water

4 tablespoons olive oil

Salt

Milk (optional)

Work together the flour and the yeast mixture, adding the oil and a pinch of salt. If you find the dough becoming too hard or not elastic enough, mix a little milk with some water and add this a little at a time until you have a soft, firm but elastic dough. Knead well. Let this rest in a cool spot, covered with a cloth, for 1 to 2 hours. Meanwhile prepare the following filling. You will need:

2 onions, sliced

4 tablespoons olive oil

1 ripe tomato, peeled and seeded (see page 23), crushed a little

Fresh basil, wiped clean with a dry cloth

4–6 anchovies, washed and cut into pieces

Garlic to taste

Black olives, pitted and halved

Sauté the onions in the oil without letting them brown, then add the tomato, stirring now and then. Add the basil leaves and the anchovies and let it cook briefly. When the dough has rested, knead it again briefly, then roll it out onto a greased baking pan so that the edges of the dough extend up the sides the width of one finger. Spread the onion mixture over the dough, and garnish with a few slices of garlic and a few black olive halves. Put in a preheated 400° oven and bake for about half an hour until golden.

64
SARDENAIRA, No. 2

Those who favor this version of the famous Ligurian pizza, also actually a *focaccia*, consider those who favor the first version traitors to their country, and vice versa. I give both versions impartially. In this version, the onions are not cooked first but instead are finely sliced and spread directly over the dough before it goes into the oven. The sauce, made without the onions, is poured over this and only black olives are used as garnish. It is baked in the same way.

You can also add a few capers to the sauce, and oregano instead of basil.

65
PIZZA RUSTICA, UMBRIAN STYLE

For 6 servings you will need:

2½ cups plus 1¾ cups flour

1 cube (⅔ ounce) compressed yeast dissolved in ½ cup water

4 eggs plus 2 yolks

¾ cup Pecorino or Romano cheese, cubed or shredded

¾ cup Parmesan cheese, grated

½ cup olive oil

Make a starter dough with 2 cups of flour and the yeast dissolved in water, adding more water little by little until you have a soft but firm dough. Let this rise in a warm place, under a cloth, for an hour. Then add the rest of the flour and about ½ cup water to make a smooth, elastic but firm dough. Knead well and spread over the pastry board. Now mix the eggs, egg yolks, Pecorino, and Parmesan together and work them all into the dough, adding olive oil little by little to make a soft but firm dough (you may not use all the oil or you may need a little more). Let this dough rest for 2 hours, covered with a cloth, in a warm place. Then roll it out and put it on a greased baking tin with high sides. Let it rest again for another hour in a warm spot. Bake in a preheated 400° oven until it is nicely browned.

This pizza is excellent eaten as is, just as it comes out of the oven, or it can be eaten garnished with black trufffles or slices of hard-boiled eggs and salami, or sliced sautéed onions.

Pizza Rustica, Umbrian Style

66
FOCACCIA, JESI STYLE

This is a traditional dish from the Marche region in central Italy. You will need:

3 cups flour
1 cube (⅔ ounce) compressed yeast
    dissolved in ½ cup warm water
Salt
2 tablespoons oil
3 eggs, beaten
¾ cups Parmesan cheese, grated
¾ cup Pecorino or Romano cheese,
    grated
½ cup Provolone cheese, cubed

Blend 1 cup of flour with the yeast dissolved in water to make a soft dough. Shape it into a ball and let it rise for at least half an hour in a warm place, covered with a cloth.

Meanwhile blend the rest of the flour with the oil, salt, and enough water to make another smooth soft dough. Add to this dough the eggs, the Parmesan, Pecorino, and Provolone, working it into the dough. Now work the two doughs together, kneading them thoroughly so that they become well blended. Put it on a greased baking pan with sides at least 1 inch high and put this in a preheated 400° oven until golden.

67
FOCACCIA WITH CHEESE, RECCO STYLE

This Ligurian *focaccia* from Recco is famous, whether it comes from Gianni Carbone of the Manuelina restaurant or from Gianni and Vittoria Bisso of the U Vittoria restaurant. This is the recipe I got from the latter. For 6 servings you will need:

> 5 cups flour
> Salt
> Water
> 1½ pounds Stracchino or farmer's cheese, sliced
> Olive oil

Blend the flour with a pinch of salt and enough water to make a smooth dough. Knead well. Let this rest in a cool spot, under a cloth, for 20 minutes. Then divide it in 2 slightly unequal parts and roll out 2 sheets, one a little larger than the other, as thin as possible, helping with your hands where necessary. Grease a large deep baking pan with oil and put in the larger sheet, which should extend a little up the sides. Spread the cheese over it and then place the second sheet on top. Press the edges together, moisten with oil, and put in a preheated 450° oven for a few minutes, until the cheese melts and the dough is golden brown.

68
FOCACCIA STUFFED WITH CHEESE

From Recco there are other versions of the *focaccia* apart from the classic one with Stracchino, and they are all very tasty. For example, you can make a filling by combining Mascarpone or cream cheese mixed with a little cream to soften it, and Gorgonzola. In this case have the bottom sheet of dough a little thicker because this is a more substantial filling. The top sheet remains as thin as possible. Bake in a preheated 450° oven.

69
FOCACCIA WITH CHEESE AND HAM OR PROSCIUTTO

As with recipe 68, the bottom sheet of dough is a little thicker and a filling is made of slices of soft cheese like farmer's cheese, with strips of ham or prosciutto.

70
FOCACCIA WITH RICOTTA AND SAUSAGE

This is similar to the others. Here the stuffing is made with 1¼ cups of Ricotta and 1½ cups of cooked sausage, cut in cubes or

Focaccia with Cheese, Recco Style

crumbled. Continue as in the previous recipes.

71
FOCACCIA WITH GREENS

This time the filling is made with spinach, beet greens, chicory or whatever greens you prefer. You will need about 6 cups of greens, boiled, drained very well, chopped and sautéed briefly in 1 tablespoon of butter. Add salt and pepper to taste. You can add Ricotta, sausage, or ham to this, or even raisins, revived in a little water, and pine nuts. The rest of the recipe is the same as in the master recipe 67.

72
FOCACCIA WITH ESCAROLE

Escarole has thick fleshy leaves with a very "green" taste and it is

Focaccia with Escarole

gether the flour, a pinch of salt, and the yeast dissolved in water, adding more water little by little until the dough is soft but firm. Knead well. Let it rest in a cool spot, under a cloth, for an hour. Meanwhile make the filling. You will need:

    4 tablespoons olive oil
    6 anchovy fillets, washed and cut into pieces
    1 cup pitted and chopped black olives
    2 tablespoons capers
    3 tablespoons raisins (optional)
    3 tablespoons pine nuts (optional)
    6 cups fresh escarole, washed, parboiled, squeezed dry, and cut in strips

Heat the olive oil in a frying pan with the anchovies, then add the olives, the capers, and finally the escarole. Let this cook 10–12 minutes over a moderate heat so that it blends well. Then, if you want to do it the traditional way, add 3 tablespoons of raisins, first revived in a little warm water and drained, and 3 tablespoons of pine nuts.

Roll the dough out into 2 sheets, one a little larger than the other. The larger one should be about ¹⁄₁₆ inch thick and it should line a greased baking pan, extending up the sides a little. Spread the filling over this, then cover with the other sheet and crimp the edges together to form a cordlike rim. Bake in a

preheated 400° oven until the crust is golden.

In a more refined version, you can use a starter dough consisting of ½ cup flour and the yeast dissolved in water, and let this rest for 1 hour, then incorporate the rest of the flour and continue as described above.

73
FOCACCIA WITH ESCAROLE AND SALT COD

This recipe is the same except for the presence of salt cod. You will need

    Dough, prepared as in recipe 72
    1½ pounds of salt cod, previously soaked, boiled, and deboned
    4 tablespoons olive oil
    2 cloves garlic, sliced
    3 tablespoons black olives, pitted and chopped
    3 tablespoons capers
    ¼ cup parsley
    6 cups fresh escarole, prepared as in recipe 72

Prepare the escarole as in the preceding recipe, and have the sheets of dough ready. Flake the cod, then sauté it briefly in the oil, adding the garlic, olives, capers and parsley. Do not use any salt. Spread half the escarole over the bottom sheet, then pour the salt cod mixture over it. Top with the rest of the escarole and cover with the top sheet. Proceed as in recipe 72.

used both cooked and raw in salads. For this rustic tart, popularly called a pizza, for 6 servings you will need:

    3½ cups flour
    Salt
    1 cube (⅔ ounce) compressed yeast dissolved in a ½ cup warm water

Make a dough by working to-

74
PIZZA WITH ONIONS, PUGLIA STYLE

Here the word "pizza" is used in its local context to indicate a kind of filled *focaccia* which is actually a sort of rustic tart. It is also called a *calzone*, but in fact the Puglian *calzone* is really a variation of this recipe. The stuffing is put on one half of the dough and the other side is folded over, forming a little rustic jewel case of flavors. For 6 servings you will need:

3½ cups flour
Salt
1 cube (⅔ ounce) compressed yeast dissolved in ½ cup warm water
3–4 tablespoons olive oil

Make a dough by working together the flour, a pinch of salt, the yeast dissolved in water, and the oil to get a smooth soft dough. Add a little more water if necessary and knead well. Let it rest at least half an hour, covered with a cloth, in a cool spot.

Meanwhile prepare the filling. You will need:

4 onions, sliced and marinated in olive oil for at least 3 hours
2 tomatoes, peeled and seeded (see page 23), crushed
¾ cup pitted and chopped black olives
3 tablespoons capers
3–6 anchovy fillets, to taste, washed and chopped

¼ cup chopped parsley
½ cup Pecorino or Romano cheese, grated

Drain the onions, then mix with the tomatoes, olives, capers, anchovies, parsley, and cheese. When the dough has risen, divide it into 2 slightly unequal pieces. Roll them out into 2 sheets, ⅟₁₆ inch thick, one a bit larger than the other. Line an oiled baking pan with the larger so that the edges extend up the side a little, spread the filling over it, and cover with the second sheet. Crimp the edges together into a ropelike rim. Moisten the top with oil and cook in a preheated 400° oven until golden brown.

If you want to save time, instead of marinating the onions you can prepare the filling by sautéing them in a few tablespoons of oil, gradually adding the other ingredients to them. When they have cooked a little, spread them over the dough.

75
PIZZA WITH ONIONS AND CHICORY

This is a very pleasing version of the Puglian pizza with onions. The filling is made as in the master recipe, but instead of adding cheese or tomatoes to the onions, you add 4 cups of chicory. If the

onions have been marinating in oil, the chicory should be boiled until tender and finely chopped before adding it to the other ingredients. However, if the onions are to be cooked, simply parboil the chicory, drain well, and chop it up before adding it to the frying pan along with the other ingredients.

76
PIZZA WITH ONIONS AND SALT COD

This is still another version of the Puglian pizza with onions as described in recipe 74. In this case, eliminate the anchovies and add 1 cup of salt cod, soaked, boiled, deboned, and cut into pieces.

Proceed as in recipe 74, spreading the filling over the bottom sheet and covering with a top sheet. Moisten with oil and put in a preheated 400° oven until the crust has turned golden brown.

77
PIZZA, CALABRIAN STYLE

This is still another version of rustic tart with onions, similar to the Puglian pizza with onions, but

Pizza with Onions, Puglia Style

123

with its own distinct identity. For 6 servings you will need:

3½ cups flour
Salt
1 cube (⅔ ounce) compressed yeast
    dissolved in ½ cup warm water
¼ cup lard
1 or 2 egg yolks

Make a dough with the flour, a pinch of salt, the yeast dissolved in water, the lard, and the egg yolks. Knead well. Let this rest while you prepare the filling. You need:

⅓ cup olive oil
3 cloves garlic, crushed but left whole
3 anchovies, washed and chopped
2 tomatoes, peeled and seeded (see
    page 23), sliced
¾ cup pitted and chopped black olives
1 can (5 ounce) tuna fish, drained

Heat the oil and brown the garlic, then discard garlic. Gradually add the other ingredients, and when they have blended together, continue as in recipe 74.

78
SCACCIATA

For this Sicilian version of onion pie, make the dough as follows. You need:

3½ cups flour
Salt
1 cube (⅔ ounce) compressed yeast
    dissolved in ½ cup warm water

Blend the flour, a pinch of salt, and the yeast dissolved in water

Focaccia, Campofranco Style

together, adding more water little by little, to get a soft but firm dough. Knead well. Let this rest for an hour in a cool spot, covered with a cloth. Then roll out 2 slightly unequal sheets to make the "pizza" as in the previous recipes. The filling is made with:

3 onions, thinly sliced
3 ounces Provolone or Caciocavallo
    cheese, thinly sliced
5–6 anchovies, washed and left whole
    or, at most, cut in two
3 ounces ham, cut into strips
¾ cup pitted and chopped black olives
1 tomato, peeled and seeded (see page
    23), sliced
Pepper

Spread these over the bottom sheet of dough, sprinkle with a little pepper, and cover with the top sheet, continuing as in recipe 74.

79
FOCACCIA, CAMPOFRANCO STYLE

For 6 servings you will need:

3½ cups flour
1½ cubes (⅔ ounce) compressed yeast
    dissolved in ½ cup warm water
3 eggs
⅓ cup butter, softened
1 pound Mozzarella cheese, sliced
½ cup tomato sauce
½ cup Parmesan cheese, grated

Make a starter dough with ½ cup of flour mixed with the yeast dissolved in water to make a very

soft dough. Let this rise for an hour, covered with a cloth. Then make a mound with the rest of the flour and make a well in the center. Put the yeast mixture in it and work it together, gradually incorporating the eggs and butter as well, adding a pinch of salt and enough water, added little by little, to make a soft but firm dough. Knead well. Spread it in a greased pan, then let it rise for half an hour.

Now, put it in a cold oven and turn it on to 300° for 40 minutes. In this way you will get a dough well cooked both inside and out. Remove from the pan at this point and cut it in half horizontally. This will give you 2 large circles or squares. Cover the lower one with a generous amount of sliced Mozzarella and then a few tablespoons of tomato sauce and a few tablespoons of grated Parmesan cheese. Cover with the top half and spread on it Mozzarella, tomato sauce, and Parmesan as well. Put in a preheated 400° oven for another 10–15 minutes so that the ingredients get hot and are well blended. Serve immediately.

In a more old-fashioned version, a few tablespoons of sugar are added to the *focaccia* dough.

125

80
FILLED TORTANO

This is still within the most traditional dishes of Neapolitan cooking. For the *tortano*, a kind of *focaccia*, for 6 servings, you will need:

2¾ cups flour
1½ cubes (⅔ ounce) compressed yeast dissolved in ½ cup warm water
3 tablespoons lard
3 tablespoons grated Parmesan cheese

Filled Tortano

Salt and pepper

Make a starter dough by blending ½ cup of flour with the yeast dissolved in water. Let this rise for at least half an hour under a cloth. Then pour the rest of the flour on a pastry board and gradually work in the risen dough, the shortening, Parmesan, salt, and a generous grinding of pepper. Add water little by little to get a soft dough. Knead well. Let it rest and rise for 2 hours in a warm spot, covered with a cloth. Meanwhile, prepare this filling. You will need:

2 cups cheese (a mixture such as Fontina, Provolone, and Bel Paese), diced
1 cup spicy sausage or salami, diced
3 hard-boiled eggs, sliced

Mix the cheeses and sausage or salami. When the dough has risen, roll it into a long rectangle with a thickness of ½ inch, and spread the filling on it, leaving a border of about ½ inch around the edge. Be sure the dough is not too thin or the filling will break through. Over the stuffing spread 3 sliced hard-boiled eggs. Now carefully roll the dough back over itself, to form a

Casatiello

long roll, like a jelly roll, pinch the seam to seal it, and then bring the ends together, forming a large ring. ·Put this, seam side down, in one piece in a greased baking pan and spread lard on the top and sides of the dough.

Let this rise for 2 hours, then bake it in a preheated 375° oven for half an hour. A very appetizing dish, served hot or cold.

81
CASATIELLO

This is a complicated but delicious recipe that also comes from traditional Neapolitan cooking. To make the dough you will need:

3½ cups flour
Salt
1¼ cups softened lard, approximately
1½ cubes (⅔ ounce) compressed yeast
    dissolved in ½ cup warm water
1 cup Parmesan cheese, grated
Pepper
3 small eggs

Blend together the flour, a pinch of salt, ¼ cup of the lard and the yeast dissolved in water, adding about ½ cup of water little by little and kneading it to get a rather soft dough. Put this dough in a bowl dusted with flour, cover with a towel, and let it rise for an hour and a half in a warm place. Then pull off an egg-sized piece of dough and set it aside. Put the rest on a pastry

board and roll it out into a long rectangle about ½ inch thick.

Spread about 2 tablespoons of the softened lard over the top of the rectangle, sprinkle with Parmesan cheese and pepper, and fold the dough in half, with the lard on the inside. Again, spread lard on the top, sprinkle with Parmesan and pepper, and fold in half. Roll the layered dough out into a rectangle the size and thickness of the original. Repeat the whole process twice, but at the end of the final time, do not roll out the dough. Instead, fold the dough so that it forms a long, narrow rectangle and shape into a roll, pressing the ends together to form a ring. Put the ring on a greased baking sheet and let the dough rise for 3 hours. Then, make three small indentations,

each one halfway into the top of the ring and evenly spaced around it to contain the eggs. Using the dough that was set aside, make strips to form rings around the indentations to hold the eggs in place. In each one break a raw egg. There is nothing left to do but put this into a preheated 300° oven for 20 minutes, then turn the heat up to 400° and bake for another 30 minutes until golden brown.

82
FITASCETTA

This is a kind of *focaccia* seasoned with onions, which is eaten in the Lake Como region. In Como, this was made with the special local dough, bought at the bakery, but you can make it yourself very easily. For 6 servings you will need:

3½ cups flour
1 cube (⅔ ounce) compressed yeast dissolved in ½ cup warm water

Mix the flour with a pinch of salt and the yeast dissolved in water. Add about ½ cup more water, little by little, until you have a very soft dough. Knead well, then let it rise, covered with a cloth, while you make the filling. You will need:

4 medium onions, sliced thin
4 tablespoons butter

Slice the onions into very thin slices, melt the butter in a pan and sauté the onions, letting them brown just a little. Now work the dough again, kneading it into a roll, and shape that into a ring, joining the two ends. Put the ring on a greased baking pan and pour the onions over the ring evenly. Put it in a preheated 400° oven and cook until the dough is golden. In older versions a little suger is sprinkled over the onions just before the ring is put in the oven.

83
SFOGLIATA

This is another version of the filled ring. For 6 servings you will need:

3½ cups flour
Salt
1 cube (⅔ ounce) compressed yeast dissolved in ½ cup warm water
½ cup olive oil

Mix the flour with a pinch of salt and the yeast dissolved in water and add the olive oil little by little to obtain a soft smooth dough. Knead it well and then let it rise for half an hour in a cool place. Meanwhile, prepare the filling. You will need:

4 medium onions, chopped
3 tablespoons olive oil
¾ cup pitted and chopped black olives

2 tomatoes, peeled and seeded (see page 23), chopped

3 anchovies, washed and chopped

1 tablespoon capers

¼ cup parsley, finely chopped

⅔ cup grated Pecorino or Romano cheese

Sauté the onions in the oil, add the olives, tomatoes, anchovies, capers, and the parsley and let them cook for a few minutes. Just before you remove the mixture from the heat, add the cheese. Stir it well to blend the flavors and set aside.

Roll out the dough into a rectangular sheet about ½ inch thick. It must be this thick or the dough will split when you roll it up. Spread some of the filling across one of the short ends, leaving a margin on each side of about 2 inches. Fold this over the filling, spread a little more of the filling over the end, and roll it again. Continue this way, filling and then rolling the dough over it until you have formed a big roll. Now shape it into a ring, bringing the ends together. Put it on a greased baking pan, moisten with a little oil, and bake it in a preheated 400° oven for about 25 minutes. When it is ready, take it out of the oven and let it cool a little before slicing. The dough can also be rolled as in a strudel.

84
SFOGLIATINE

Using the same quantities of the same ingredients you can divide the dough up and make six or eight small *sfogliate*, which are then called *sfogliatine*. More often, though, a simpler stuffing is used, made of chopped green olives, chopped anchovies, olive oil, salt and pepper. These are mixed, uncooked, and then spread over the sheet and rolled up as in the *sfogliate*, before putting it in the oven. This should also cool a little before cutting it.

Sfogliata

129

85
FOCACCIA WITH MOZZARELLA, No. 1

This is an old Neapolitan tradition. For 6 servings you will need:

6 slices dark bread, home-made style, about ½ inch thick
Butter or lard
1¾ pounds Mozzarella cheese, sliced
¼ cup parsley, chopped, or fresh basil
2 eggs, beaten
Pepper

Grease a baking pan, large enough to hold the bread slices very close together, touching but not overlapping and leaving no empty spaces. Cover these slices with slices of Mozzarella, again leaving no space uncovered. The cheese can overlap a little. Garnish with the parsley or basil, cover with the beaten eggs and a sprinkling of freshly ground pepper, and put in a preheated 400° oven for 20 minutes. A nice golden crust forms on the bread that becomes crisp and savory.

A variation is to sprinkle small bits of anchovy, washed first to remove some of the saltiness, over the slices of Mozzarella.

86
FOCACCIA WITH MOZZARELLA, No. 2

This is a red version of *focaccia* with Mozzarella, because it uses tomatoes. You will need 6 or more peeled and seeded tomatoes (see page 23), cut in wedges and spread over the Mozzarella. The rest is the same as version 1.

87
FOCACCIA WITH POTATOES

This *focaccia* is a delicious morsel from the Neapolitan kitchen made with a very special dough. For 6 servings you will need:

3½ cups flour
Salt
1–2 medium potatoes, boiled and mashed with no additions
1 cube (⅔ ounce) compressed yeast dissolved in ½ cup warm water

Add a pinch of salt to the flour and then mix it with the potato and the yeast dissolved in water. Add more water, little by little, until you have a rather soft dough. Knead well. Let this dough rest about an hour, covered with a cloth. Then roll out 6 circles, no more than ¼ inch thick. Put them on a greased baking sheet, garnish to taste (any pizza recipe will work fine) and put in a preheated 350° oven for 20–30 minutes.

Focaccia with Potatoes

88
TORTA RUSTICA WITH GREENS

The *torta rustica* is a rustic tart which only uses one sheet of dough. This is laid out on a baking pan and the filling is spread over it

before it is put in the oven; there is no top sheet. To make the dough you will need:

3½ cups flour
Salt
1 cube (⅔ ounce) compressed yeast dissolved in ½ cup warm water
6 cups fresh greens (spinach, beet, chicory), steamed, drained, and chopped
¾ cup Ricotta cheese

Olive oil
Salt and pepper

Add a pinch of salt to the flour and make the dough by mixing the flour and yeast dissolved in water, adding about ½ cup more water, little by little, until you have a soft but elastic dough. Knead this dough a few minutes, then shape it into a ball and cut a cross into the

top of the dough. Cover with a cloth and let it rise in a warm place for at least half an hour and up to 2 hours if you have the time. Then knead it again and spread it over a greased baking pan so it is about ¼ inch thick and large enough to extend up the sides a little. You can spread whatever greens are in season on it, mixed with the

Ricotta and a pinch of salt and pepper. Moisten the pie with a little oil and put it in a preheated 350° oven for about 30–45 minutes.

A variation of this is to sauté the boiled and chopped greens first in 2 or 3 tablespoons of oil, along with a little pepper and a few pieces of anchovy. Or you can make a *soffritto* by sautéing a little finely chopped onion in oil with some bits of anchovy and then add the boiled and chopped greens to it before spreading it on the dough.

Torta Rustica with Onions and Tomatoes

89
TORTA RUSTICA WITH ONIONS AND TOMATOES

Prepare the dough as in the master recipe 88. For the filling you will need:

6 onions, thinly sliced
Olive oil
Salt and pepper
¼ cup chopped parsley
1 teaspoon thyme
1 tablespoon fresh mint, chopped, or ½ teaspoon dried (optional)
2 eggs, beaten
¼ cup cream
½ cup breadcrumbs (approximately)
6 tomatoes, peeled and seeded (see page 23), sliced

Sauté the onions in a little oil until they are translucent. Add

salt, pepper, parsley, thyme, and mint. Remove from heat and add the eggs, cream, and enough breadcrumbs to make a soft but not fluid mixture. Line a large baking pan with the dough as in the preceding recipe, and over it spread first the onions and then the tomatoes. Moisten with a little fresh oil and bake in a preheated 350° oven for about 45 minutes.

90
TORTA RUSTICA WITH SPINACH OR BEET GREENS

For 6 servings you will need:

Dough, as in the master recipe 88
6 cups spinach or beet greens
3 eggs
1 cup Ricotta cheese
½ cup Parmesan cheese, grated
3 anchovy fillets, washed
Pepper
Olive oil

Parboil the spinach in a small amount of water, drain it very well, and chop it up finely. Beat the eggs and add the spinach, then the cheeses, the anchovies, and a little freshly grated pepper. Mix well to blend the flavors. Have the dough ready as in recipe 88. Spread the mixture over it, moisten with a little oil, and bake in a preheated 350° oven for about 45 minutes.

*Torta Rustica with Spinach
or Beet Greens*

91
TORTA RUSTICA WITH RICOTTA AND CHEESE

Prepare the dough as in the master recipe 88. For the filling you will need:

1¼ cups Ricotta cheese
2 cups Gruyère or Fontina cheese, cubed
6 egg yolks
Salt and pepper
2 tablespoons butter, melted

Mix the cheeses, the egg yolks, salt, pepper, and the melted butter together to get a soft but well-blended filling. Fill and bake the *torta rustica* following the instructions in recipe 88.

92
TORTA RUSTICA WITH HAM AND MOZZARELLA

Prepare the dough as in the master recipe 88. Make the filling with:

8 ounces diced ham or 4 ounces ham and 4 ounces salami
1½ cups Mozzarella or smoked Provolone cheese or a combination, diced

3 eggs
Salt and pepper
Oregano
3 tablespoons milk or melted butter

Mix the ham and cheese together. Beat the eggs and pour over the ham and cheese. Season with salt, pepper, and a pinch of oregano and add the milk or butter by the spoonful to bind the mixture and get just the right consistency, not too dry and not too moist. Then continue as in recipe 88.

133

93
PANDORATO, No. 1

This is an Italian version of French toast. For 6 servings, you will need:

6 slices Italian bread, about ½ inch thick

¾ cup lukewarm milk
3 eggs beaten
Salt and pepper

Arrange the slices of bread in a single layer in the milk in a shallow pan. Cover with the beaten eggs and sprinkle with salt and pepper. Let the bread soak for about an hour and then fry each slice in a generous amount of olive oil. When the *pandorato* are golden on both sides, remove from the pan and drain well. Sprinkle with salt and pepper and serve hot.

Pandorato, No. 1

94
PANDORATO, No. 2

This is the same as the first recipe, except that you make a small slit in the side of each slice of bread with the tip of a knife and in it you insert a little piece of Mozzarella and anchovy. Then

soak it in the milk and egg and continue as in the first version.

95
FARINATA, No. 1

This time chick-pea flour enters the picture. This humble but tasty and colorful dish is part of the traditional cooking of Liguria. The most common recipe, serving 6, calls for:

> 3¾ cups chick-pea flour
> 6 cups water
> ⅓ cup olive oil
> Pepper

Mix the flour and water together with a little salt to get a very fluid batter. This must rest 12 hours, usually overnight. After it has rested, carefully remove the skin that will have formed on the top. Stir what is left.

Now pour olive oil in a large baking pan and spread it around well. Pour the *farinata* batter over this and blend it so that the oil is absorbed. The batter should be about ½ inch deep. Bake this in a preheated 475° oven, and when the top becomes a rather dark golden yellow it is done. Let it cool a little and serve it cut into pieces. It is often served with a little pepper sprinkled over it.

96
FARINATA, No. 2

In a variation typical of the western Ligurian Riviera, sprinkle

thinly sliced raw onions over the dough before baking.

97
FARINATA, No. 3

In another variation, the *farinata* is thicker, at least 1 inch, and chopped rosemary is spread over it.

98
PANICCIA

This is a Piedmont version of the *farinata*, made with chick-pea flour. Heat 6 cups of water to the simmering point, then, away from the heat, stir while slowly pouring 3¾ cups of chick-pea flour into it. Put it back on the heat, stirring constantly so that it forms a rather solid dough, like polenta. Pour this hot dough onto a pastry board or large plate, forming a circle about ½ inch thick. Spread a little olive oil and some chopped onions on top, add salt and pepper, slice, and serve immediately.

99
PANELLE

The *panelle* are very simple food from Sicily, or, more exactly, Palermo. Carefully made, it is very appetizing. For 6 servings you will need:

4 cups chick-pea flour
Olive oil

Pour enough water in a pan with the chick-pea flour to make a very thick but fluid batter. Bring this to a boil and cook it until you have a creamy substance. Pour it over a mable slab wiped with oil so that the batter is ¹⁄₁₆ inch thick. Let this cool, then cut it into various shapes. Heat a generous amount of oil (about ½ inch) and fry the *panelle* in this until golden brown. Serve hot.

100
GRISSINI

Grissini, which are just about the thinnest form of bread known, can also be made at home. They come from the Piedmont region and date back to the seventeenth century. A kind of light salty cracker, they add a touch of elegance to any table. You will need:

3½ cups flour
Salt
1 cube (⅔ ounce) compressed yeast dissolved in ½ cup tepid water
3–4 tablespoons oil
Milk

Add a pinch of salt to the flour and mix in the yeast dissolved in water, the oil, and then enough milk, added little by little, to make a soft but firm dough. Knead well. Let this dough rest for half an hour, then knead it again briefly and divide it into small pieces. Roll out each piece into a long thin strip, to the length and thickness you prefer. Grease a lage baking sheet with oil and spread these strips on it. Bake in a preheated 400° oven for 10–15 minutes until they become crisp and golden with a flaky texture.

Sometimes aromatic herbs like rosemary are blended into the dough or even finely chopped onions or garlic or whatever your taste and imagination inspire you to add.

101
SCHIACCIATE WITH RICOTTA

These are a kind of cheese wafer and for 6 servings you will need:

2 cups flour
Salt
1 cup Ricotta cheese
½ cup butter, softened

Add a pinch of salt to the flour, then blend the flour and Ricotta together, and finally add the butter. Knead it to get a soft homogenous dough, taking care not to overwork it. It should not be too elastic. Roll it out into a sheet ¹⁄₁₆ inch thick and cut as many circles from that as you can, 2½–3 inches in diameter. Put these circles on a greased baking sheet and put them in a preheated 425° oven for about 10 minutes. You can eat them as they are, but you can also use them as a base for a delicious little tart by covering them with sardines, tuna, salmon, herring, or even salami or ham.

Panelle

102
TORTA PASQUALINA

This is a puff-pastrylike dough with a spinach and Ricotta filling that has eggs embedded in it. It is called an Easter Torte because it is traditionally served at that time of year. In Liguria it is still a central part of the Easter ritual; the vegetables and eggs symbolize the return of life in the spring. It is a dish requiring time and patience and therefore it is made less frequently now. Attempts to simplify or modify it have often proved disappointing. But although it is time consuming, it is well worth the effort. The original recipe is given below with the advice that it is best made for many people. For the dough you will need:

 9 cups flour
 Salt
 4 tablespoons olive oil
 2½–3 cups water

Add a pinch of salt to the flour and then knead the flour with the olive oil and enough water, added little by little, to make a soft but smooth dough. Divide this dough into 14 equal portions and set them aside on a floured cloth, covered with a dampened cloth. For the filling you will need:

 2 pounds (8–10 cups) spinach, washed well and steamed
 3 tablespoons grated Parmesan cheese
 Salt

Torta Pasqualina

138

2½ cups Ricotta cheese
2 tablespoons flour
¾ cup cream
12 small eggs
Olive oil
Butter, melted
Parmesan cheese, grated
Oil

Squeeze the excess water out of the spinach and chop it roughly. Mix it in a bowl with the Parmesan and a pinch of salt. Set aside. In another bowl, combine the Ricotta, flour, and cream, adding salt to taste.

Now, roll out 13 of the 14 portions into circles that will fit inside a deep baking dish with sides 2 inches high. The last portion should be rolled out so that it is large enough to go up the sides and extend slightly over the rim.

Grease the dish and lay the larger piece of dough inside, letting it extend up over the edge. Brush it with oil, then lay one of the other circles on top. Brush that one with oil and continue layering the dough, one on top of the other, always brushing each one until you have seven layers.

On top of the last layer, spread the spinach mixture. Dribble a little oil over it. Then pour the ricotta mixture over that. Make 12 small wells in the filling with the bowl of a spoon and break a small egg into each one. Put a small spoonful of melted butter, a pinch of salt, and a bit of grated cheese on top of each egg.

Now very gently cover this with another circle of dough and brush a little oil on top of it. Continue to layer and brush with oil until all the layers have been used. The top layer should be brushed too, and then the edges sealed by pinching the top and bottom layers together. Prick the top with a fork so the steam can escape during cooking.

Bake in a preheated 375° oven for 1 hour. Serve either warm or cool, never hot.

Steamed and chopped artichokes may be substituted for the spinach. In this case use only the most tender leaves and the heart.

103
NECCI

These humble yet delicious *schiacciatine*, made of chestnut flour, come from Tuscany. It was not so long ago that the chestnut was an important source of food for the poor mountain folk in the Apennines and the Alps. They were served whole, boiled or roasted, seasoned with milk or wine or mixed with other ingredients. Chestnuts were also ground into flour, and made into a kind of bread, the recipe for which follows. You will need:

3¾ cups chestnut flour
Pinch of salt
½ cup cold water

Necci

Make a dough with the chestnut flour, salt, and water, adding flour little by little until you get a rather stiff but still malleable dough. You may need more water or you may use less, it is only a relative amount. Shape the *schiacciate* into round flat shapes and bake them on a greased sheet in a preheated 400° oven for about 10 minutes.

Traditionally *necci* are made with a special utensil, which has a pair of hinged jaws on a long handle. The dough is put inside the jaws, giving it its traditional round flattened shape, and then is exposed directly to the fire, which should be made from aromatic wood, preferably on the family hearth, for a few minutes. And it is traditionally accompanied by Ricotta, fresh from the summer mountain huts. It's true that it can be hard to find all these things — the hearth, the implements, the chestnut flour — but even cooked on an ordinary baking sheet in an ordinary oven, it's worth the effort of tackling the job.

104
CASTAGNACCIO

The *castagnaccio* can also be considered a sweet, in fact, the sweet most beloved by children (at least it was several decades ago). It was sold steaming hot on the streets in the fall, savory and friendly, at this very difficult time of year when you had to go back to school and

the cold was beginning to redden your nose.

But the *castagnaccio* is not just a sweet, otherwise it would not be included in this book. It is more, a complete food, in which the sweet taste, very limited in this version, mixed with the other ingredients in wonderful harmony. For 6 servings you will need:

3¾ cups chestnut flour, sifted so it has no lumps
Salt
½ cup of water, approximately
1½ teaspoons fennel seed
2 tablespoons pine nuts
¼ cup raisins

Mix the chestnut flour in a bowl with water seasoned with a pinch of salt, adding the flour little by little, using a ladle or whisk to get a thick batter. Pour this batter in a deep pie dish that you have greased well and on top sprinkle fennel seeds, pine nuts, and raisins, revived in warm water, and moisten the top with oil. Bake this in a preheated 400° oven until the top has formed a nice crust. Eat the *castagnaccio* lukewarm or cold.

Note: The version of *castagnaccio* just described is from Liguria. There is also a Tuscan version that adds olive oil and sugar to the dough and sprinkles rosemary leaves with the pine nuts and raisins on top. It is this Tuscan version which can really be classified as a sweet.

Castagnaccio

105
FRISEDDE

This is a toasted bread typical of Puglia; it goes well with peasant dishes. For 6 servings you will need:

5 cups flour
Salt
1½ cubes (⅔ ounce) compressed yeast dissolved in ½ cup warm water

Add a pinch of salt to the flour then add the yeast dissolved in water, adding about ½ cup more water, little by little, as necessary to make a breadlike dough. Knead well. Divide this dough into little balls, then roll each one out into a snake and shape it into a ring. Take two rings and put one on top of the other, pressing them together a little so that they stick. Continue with the others. Let them rest like this for half an hour and then bake on an oiled pan in a preheated 375° oven. Watch them carefully while they bake, and when they are about halfway cooked, take them out and separate them where they were joined — in Puglia this is done with an iron wire — and put them back in the oven to finish baking.

The *frisedde* are served as a cakelike bread. In Puglia they are moistened with a little water to soften them, without making them soggy, then covered with fresh crushed tomatoes, a sprinkling of salt and oregano, and a little green flavorful olive oil over all.

PART THREE

Other recipes from around the world

1
PITA

This is another form of *schiacciata* which puffs up when it bakes so that it opens up like a pocket when you cut it horizontally. It is found in many parts of the Mediterranean, including Sicily. It goes by many names but it seems fairest to use its Arabic name since it is so common in the Middle East. For 6 servings you will need:

> 3½ cups flour
> Salt
> 1 cube (⅔ ounce) compressed yeast
>   dissolved in ½ cup warm water

Make a dough by adding a pinch of salt to the flour, then the yeast dissolved in the water, adding more water, little by little, as necessary to get a soft dough. Knead well. This dough should be left to rise in a wide, shallow bowl or pan for at least 2½ hours; 3 is even better. When the time has passed, punch down the dough. Pull off pieces of dough and shape each into a relatively thick circle. Put them in the preheated 450° oven for 8–10 minutes. When they are golden brown, they will be puffed up like little pillows. They can be cut across the top and filled with different things. The most common is to fill them with balls of chick-peas, mashed and mixed with other ingredients, called *felafel,* but you can also use Ricotta or a creamy cheese, boiled and

chopped greens, or whatever suits your fancy.

2
CHAPATI

This bread is from India and Southeast Asia and it greatly resembles a pizza, suggesting that they both had similar origins. For 6 servings you will need:

> 4½ cups flour, preferably whole wheat
> Salt
> 4 tablespoons butter, softened
> 1 cup water, approximately

Add a pinch of salt to the flour and work in the butter and enough water, added little by little, to make a soft, smooth dough. Knead it until it is elastic, then shape it into a ball and let it rest in a cool place, covered with a damp cloth, for an hour. Knead it again briefly and divide it into smaller pieces. Roll them out into circles ¹⁄₁₆ inch thick. Grease a baking sheet with butter or oil, and bake the *chapati* in a preheated 425° oven until they are golden brown on both sides. When the dough is made correctly, the circles will tend to puff up a little, with one side puffed up slightly more than the other.

These *chapati* are used either like bread to accompany various foods, or as little plates which soak up the juices of the food put on top. Bread was used in the same way in the West, up to the Middle Ages and beyond. There is no tradition of garnishing the *chapati* with dif-

ferent seasonings as we do with our pizza, though it is often served covered with onions and other vegetables, minced fine, and eaten like that.

3
PARATHAS

Parathas are very similar to *chapati* and they are equally wide-

Chapati

spread in India and other places in Southeast Asia. Relative to the *chapati*, they are a richer, softer bread and are kneaded longer. For 6 servings, you will need:

4½ cups flour
Salt
2 tablespoons softened butter
2–3 ounces melted butter
1 cup water, approximately

Add a pinch of salt to the flour, blend the flour, 2 tablespoons of softened butter, and as much water as necessary to make a smooth, firm dough. Knead it until it is somewhat elastic then let it rest in a cool spot for an hour, covered with a slightly damp cloth. After an hour, knead it again briefly, then divide it into balls of dough. Flat-ten each one into a circle about 1/16 inch thick and brush each circle with lukewarm melted butter. Fold it in half and brush it with more butter, then fold it into quarters, brushing one more time with the butter. Roll this little bundle out again to form it back into a circle

147

about $\frac{1}{16}$ inch thick. Bake on a baking sheet in a preheated 400° oven until golden brown.

4
POORI

Besides the *chapati*, a kind of pancake is eaten in India called *poori*. For 6 servings you will need:

3½ cups of flour
Salt
1½ cubes (⅔ ounce) compressed yeast dissolved in ½ cup water
2 tablespoons butter
Oil

Add a pinch of salt to the flour and then blend the flour, the yeast dissolved in water, and butter, adding about ½ cup more water as necessary to form a soft but firm dough. Knead it until it is smooth and let it rest for half an hour, under a cloth. Then knead it again and divide it into smaller balls of dough. Flatten them into circles about 6 inches in diameter and $\frac{1}{16}$ inch thick. Fry them on a hot oiled skillet until golden on both sides. This takes very little time because they puff up almost right away. Drain them well on absorbent paper and serve immediately, while still very hot.

5
STUFFED POORI

Make the circles of dough as above, simply a little thicker and about 4 inches in diameter. The

filling can be made in many ways, for example, mixing mashed potatoes and onions sautéed in butter with a little ginger and aromatic herbs, or hot peppers, or you can mix minced chicken with an egg and cream. Another idea is to combine chopped boiled greens with sautéed onions, or eggs and cheese. The stuffing is put on half the dough and then the other half is folded over it, pinching the edges together to seal, and the *poori* is fried on a hot skillet, generously oiled.

6
DOSHA WITH LENTILS AND RICE

To make these delightful Indian pancakes, you will need:

    10 ounces lentils
    ½ cup rice
    1 cube (⅔ ounce) compressed yeast
        dissolved in ½ cup warm water
    Paprika

Separately soak the rice and the lentils in water to cover for 12 hours. Puree each in a blender. Mix the rice and the lentils together and add the yeast and a generous sprinkling of paprika, adding a little more water if necessary to get a rather fluid batter. Let this batter rest for half an hour, and then drop

Stuffed Poori

149

by spoonfuls onto a hot, oiled skillet and fry until golden on both sides.

7
LOOKI

This is a kind of Bengali pancake similar to the *poori*. For 6 servings you will need:

3½ cups flour
Salt
1 tablespoon butter, softened

Add a pinch of salt to the flour and blend it with the butter and enough water, added little by little, to make a soft, smooth dough. Knead it a little then divide it into balls and flatten them on a floured board to form flat circles about 5 inches in diameter. Fry them in ¼ inch of hot oil, turning them over until they are crisp and golden on both sides. Drain well. They are delicious hot or cold.

8
POLISH-STYLE PANCAKES

These little pancakes are cooked, wrapped around a meat filling, and then fried. You will need:

2 cups flour
3 eggs, beaten
1 cup milk, approximately
Salt
Butter

Polish-Style Pancakes

Mix flour and eggs, adding a pinch of salt. Add milk little by little until you have a thick but smooth batter. Let it rest for an hour. Melt butter in a skillet and drop the batter in by spoonfuls. Do not let these little pancakes brown. Drain them and spread them on a cutting board. On each one put a

filling made as follows:

8 ounces cooked meat, minced or ground
3 eggs, beaten
2–3 onions, chopped fine
Salt and pepper
1 egg, beaten
Breadcrumbs

Combine the first three ingredients, add salt and pepper to taste, then put a spoonful on each pancake and roll up the pancake. Pinch the ends of each roll together to close them, and dip each one in a little beaten egg and then in bread-crumbs. Finish cooking them in a frying pan with a little butter until browned and crispy on the outside.

9 EGGPLANT FRITTERS

As with so many curious delicacies, this simple eggplant fritter comes from China. For 6 servings you will need:

3 or 4 eggplants, peeled and cut into pieces
4½ cups flour
5 eggs, beaten
2 onions, finely chopped
2 tablespoons soy sauce
Salt
½ teaspoon powdered ginger
¼ cup sake or dry Marsala

Put the pieces of eggplant into a blender or food processor, then put the pulp that you get through a food mill or sieve. Set this puree aside. Now make a dough, mixing together first the flour and beaten eggs, then adding the remaining ingredients and the eggplant puree, mixing until you have an homogenous batter. If it is too stiff, add a little water. Heat a gener-

ously oiled iron skillet, then drop big spoonfuls of the batter into the hot oil, shaping them as you go. Cook until they are brown on both sides, then drain on absorbent paper and serve hot.

Eggplant Fritters

10
FISH DUMPLINGS

This recipe comes from the heart regions of Africa. It begins with a dough made with:

3½ cups flour
Salt
1 cube (⅔ ounce) compressed yeast dissolved in ½ cup warm water

Add a pinch of salt to the flour and mix with the yeast and water. Add about ½ cup more water, little by little, as necessary, to get a firm but soft dough. Knead well and let rest for half an hour in a cool place, covered with a cloth. Meanwhile prepare the filling:

14 ounces fish, poached and then minced
2 onions, sliced thin
2 cloves garlic, crushed
1 green pepper, pounded in a mortar or ground in blender or food processor
½ cup breadcrumbs soaked in milk, then drained
Salt and pepper

Combine the filling ingredients and add salt and pepper to taste. When the dough has rested for half an hour, roll it out and cut into 6-inch squares. Divide the filling up among the squares, putting a little on half the square then folding the other half over it. Pinch the edges together. Fry these dumplings in ½ inch of hot oil.

Fritters with Shrimp

These dumplings are often served in their own land with a hot sauce made by sautéing a chopped onion until it is translucent, then adding a little tomato pulp and a little chopped or minced hot pepper, with salt and pepper to taste.

11
FRITTERS WITH SHRIMP

This is a Vietnamese dish. For 6 servings you will need:

1½ pounds shrimp, peeled and minced fine
8 ounces fatback, finely minced
Flour for dredging
Lard or butter

Mix the shrimp well with the fatback, and shape into small balls. Dredge in flour and fry in either lard or butter over medium-high heat. In the Orient they are held tightly between two sticks of aromatic wood and put directly over the fire of a brazier. They are moistened every so often with a little melted butter during cooking.

They are often served dipped in a sauce called *nuoc-mam*, made by marinating fish and fish entrails with oil, hot peppers, and spices. You can make a very appetizing sauce much more quickly with oil, mashed anchovies, and hot peppers.

12
SCONES

For 6 servings you will need:

2 cups flour
¾ cup softened butter
1 cube (⅔ ounce) compressed yeast dissolved in ½ cup warm water
Salt
3–4 tablespoons milk

Work the ingredients together, adding the milk little by little to get a soft dough. Knead well. Let it rest at least 1 hour in a bowl covered with a cloth. Then roll out a sheet of dough on the pastry board to a thickness of ½ inch. Cut out as many circles, about 3 inches in diameter, as you can. Spread them on a greased sheet and put them in a preheated 400° oven for 15 minutes. They will rise during baking. When they are done, cut them in half and spread with butter. Serve immediately.

13
BLINI, No. 1

These are the famous Russian pancakes that often accompany caviar, though they are also served with other garnishes. For 6 servings you will need:

2½ cups flour
3½ cups milk
2 eggs
Salt
Oil or butter

Mix the first four ingredients together to make a thin batter. Drop it by spoonfuls onto a hot griddle greased with a little oil or butter. The pancakes will take shape and cook quickly, and since they are so thin they do not even need to be turned over. When they have cooked, they are ready to serve. Often melted butter or sour cream, chopped onion, and chopped hard-boiled egg are served with them, as well as caviar.

14
BLINI, No. 2

Prepare the blini as in recipe 13. As each blini is ready, spread it with a little filling made with crumbled fresh cheese or Ricotta, mixed with an egg, cream, and if you wish, sugar, cinnamon and raisins for a sweet version. When they are filled, either roll them around the filling or fold them like

little envelopes and sauté them briefly in a little butter.

napkin to keep warm until serving. Add more oil to the skillet as necessary.

15
BLINI, No. 3

Prepare the blini as in recipe 13. Then spread them in layers in a pan greased with butter, alternating with layers of apple slices and little bits of butter. You can also sprinkle sugar, cinnamon, and powdered clove for a sweet version. Put this *blini* "torte" in a preheated 375° oven for half an hour.

16
PANCAKES

For 6 servings you will need:

1½ cups flour
2 eggs
1¾ cups milk or buttermilk

Blend the ingredients together to get a smooth liquid batter. Let it rest for half an hour. Heat just a tablespoon of oil in a skillet. Pour the batter in by spoonfuls to form the pancakes. Adjust the heat of the skillet as necessary so the pancakes don't burn. Turn them over when small bubbles break on the surface and they lose their wet appearance. When both sides are golden brown, they are ready; put them in a basket covered with a

Blini, No. 2 (left)
Pancakes (right)

Tortilla

17
TORTILLA

This is the Mexican version of *schiacciata* or *focaccia*, handed down from the ancient Indian civilizations. Tortillas are made of corn flour and still serve as bread in Mexico. They were first used in religious rituals, and it was the custom of the ancient Aztecs to prepare the *tortillas* with a little human blood from the sacrifices made to please their gods.

They would first wash the dried corn, then boil it in plenty of water with a little lime juice until the outer skin began to peel off. The corn was then removed from the fire, drained, and left to cool. Then the skins were removed, a job requiring the patience of a saint, and the kernels washed again in cold water. This formed a soft mass called *nixtamal*. The *nixtamal* was then pounded and mashed to get a soft, homogenous meal called *masa*. The prepared corn flour is called *masa harina* and can be found in stores selling Mexican or gourmet products. Today *tortillas* are also made of wheat flour, but these are not quite the same. For 6 servings you will need:

2½ cups corn flour (*masa harina*)
Salt
1½ cups cold water, approximately

Green Enchiladas

Mix a pinch of salt with the corn flour and start to add the water in a steady stream, stirring constantly. Add just enough water to form a malleable dough. Divide the dough into balls and flatten each with floured hands or a tortilla press until you have a flat circle no more than 1/16 inch thick.

The *tortillas* are cooked on clay or metal disks, like the Italian *piadine* or *tigelle*, or directly on a medium-hot ungreased griddle, until they are dry looking and beginning to brown. They cook very quickly and should be put in a basket covered with a napkin so they do not cool off too much before they are served. They replace bread and can go with any food.

18
GREEN ENCHILADAS

These are a celebrated use of *tortillas*. For 6 servings you will need:

12 thin *tortillas* (recipe 17)
12 medium-hot peppers, like the California green chile
2 eggs
½ cup milk
Salt
Chopped onion
Monterey Jack cheese, grated

Roast the chile peppers, then

peel them. Plunge them in boiling water for a second and then pound them into a paste. Mix the eggs with the milk and a pinch of salt. Dip each *tortilla* in the milk-egg batter, coating both sides, then fry it in a little melted butter or fatback. Drain well, and in the middle of each *tortilla* put a little of the mashed pepper. Wrap the *tortilla* around it, forming a roll, put it on a serving plate and sprinkle generously with the onion and grated cheese.

19
RED ENCHILADAS

Another variation using the Mexican *tortilla*. For 6 servings you will need:

12 thin *tortillas*
2 tomatoes
6 green chile peppers like the California green chile
1½ cups roast pork, chopped fine
1 cup Monterey Jack cheese, shredded
½ cup cream
2 eggs

Parboil the tomatoes, peel and seed them (see page 23). Roast and peel the peppers. Chop both up fine and mix well. Add the chopped pork and the cheese. Separately beat the eggs and add the cream. Soak the *tortillas* in the cream-egg mixture, then fry them in butter or melted fatback and drain well. On each *tortilla* spread a little of the filling, and roll the tortilla up to form a large tube. Serve covered with more cheese.

20
BRIK WITH EGGS

The name of this dish, common in Morocco, Algeria, and Tunisia, comes from the Turkish word *beurrek*. But the differences between *brik* and its Turkish counterpart (see recipes 24 and 25) are substantial, beginning with the dough. Proper equipment is necessary, as is a certain amount of skill. The dough is called *malsuca*. To make it you will need 1 cup of semolina (hard-grained flour).

Work the semolina together with a pinch of salt and enough water to make a soft dough. Let it rest under a cloth for 1 hour. Then work it again, adding more liquid until it becomes very soft but still cohesive. This dough should be cooked a small amount at a time, but in a very different way from the classic crêpe.

Traditionally it is made on a curious leather tray with a convex tin bottom, which is placed over a small brazier. When you are ready to begin, you take a ball of dough in your hand and let it drop on the heated tray bottom. The moment it touches the tray the dough is removed, so only a very thin film stays on the metal. This is then gently taken off and allowed to cool and dry. Continue this way until you have as many ready as you need. Then make the filling. For 6 servings you will need:

2 small onions
Parsley, chopped
Salt and pepper
6 eggs

Parboil the onions, then slice them, adding the parsley, salt and pepper to taste. Divide this up among six *briks*, and in the center

Brik with Eggs

Brik with Potatoes and Eggs

of each break an egg. Fold one side over the other carefully, keeping the egg inside, and lightly pinch the edges together. Then gently place it into a skillet coated with hot olive oil and fry it until it is golden on both sides. The cooking won't take long and the *brik* should be served immediately. The egg inside stays soft, so you must be careful not to spill it on yourself when you bite into it. (It is an old joke, at the expense of the ignorant, to give someone a *brik* for the first time with no advance warning and watch the egg spill out on him. Picasso loved to play this trick on the unsuspecting.) The whole process can, of course, be simplified using a more traditional pancake or phyllo dough, and also by eliminating Picasso's joke.

21
BRIK WITH POTATOES AND EGGS

This is another popular version of the *brik*. For the filling you will need:

3 potatoes, boiled, peeled, and mashed
1 onion, chopped
3 hard-boiled eggs, chopped
¼ cup parsley, minced
2 tablespoons capers
Salt and pepper
1 tablespoon grated lemon peel

Mix the ingredients well and divide the filling among the *brik*. Proceed as in the previous recipe.

22
BRIK WITH MEAT

For this filling you will need:

1½ cups boiled or roasted meat, chopped fine or pounded to a paste
3 hard-boiled eggs, crumbled
1 onion, chopped
¼ cup parsley, minced

Mix these ingredients and divide them among the *brik*. Continue as in recipe 20.

23
FISH BRIK

For this filling you can use fish, shellfish, or even a mixture of fish. You can also add crumbled hard-boiled eggs, chopped onions, parsley, salt and pepper, and if necessary, a drop of oil to soften it. Follow recipe 20.

Beurrek, No. 1

24
BEURREK, No. 1

This Turkish dish, similar to the Arab *brik*, suggests a kind of fried pizza with a meat filling. We don't know who made it first, but today a similar name is given to similar little pizzas in Muslim North Africa, and the Italian word *buricchi* refers to a kind of pizza made by the Jewish community of Ferrara. This suggests that it may have been the Jews from the East who brought this recipe with them, spreading it to the places they settled in throughout the Mediterranean.

For 6 servings you will need:

2½ cups flour
Salt
6 egg yolks
Water

Make a dough with the flour, a pinch of salt, the egg yolks, and as much water as you need, worked in a little at a time to make a very soft dough. Let this rest in a cool spot for 1 hour, covered with a cloth. Then roll it out as thinly as possible with a rolling pin and your hands. Form ovals from the sheet, 5 inches long and 2 inches wide. Rectangles also work here.

For the filling you will need:

1½ cups of Ricotta cheese
2 cups of cream
Salt and pepper
Melted butter
2 egg yolks
Breadcrumbs
Olive oil

Mix the cheese, cream, salt, and pepper until well blended. Then brush each oval with butter and

Beurrek, No. 2

place a lump of filling on one half. Fold the dough over and seal the edges. Using your finger or the handle of a wooden spoon held lengthwise, make indentations across the width of the *beurrek*. The final effect should be that the filling forms little waves under the dough. Pinch the open edges together, brush the surface with egg yolk, sprinkle with breadcrumbs, and fry in plenty of hot olive oil.

25
BEURREK, No. 2

Follow the same method in this version, but add roasted or boiled lamb and a hard-boiled egg, both chopped finely, to the cheese and cream along with aromatic herbs like thyme or cinnamon and allspice. If you make this filling with beef or veal in combination with the other ingredients, you will have *buricchi*, Ferrara style.

26
MEAT PIROSHKI, No. 1

This dish, characteristic of the Russian and Polish kitchens, can be classified as a type of *pizzette*. The dough is rolled out and cut into pieces and different fillings are placed on them. Then they are baked. (There also exist true dumplings, which are boiled and seasoned in various ways.) For 6 servings you will need:

163

1¼ cups flour
Salt
1 egg, beaten
½ cup butter

Make a dough mixing the flour, a pinch of salt, the beaten egg, and enough water to make a smooth, firm, but pliable dough. Knead well. Shape it into a ball and let it rest for half an hour, covered with a cloth. Meanwhile work butter to soften it and shape it into a ball.

Sprinkle ¾ cup of flour on the pastry board and spread the dough over it, pressing it with the rolling pin so that it absorbs the dry flour. Shape this dough into a square about 1 inch thick. On top put the ball of butter, crush it a little, then wrap it with the dough. Flatten the dough with the rolling pin again, but do not work it or knead it. Form another square, again 1 inch thick. Now, let this rest two or three minutes, then fold the square over on itself and roll it out with the rolling pin. Let it rest again, then fold it again and roll it out. Do this at least five times; seven is better. The last time, roll the dough out so that it is ¼ inch thick. Cut this sheet into 4-inch squares and set aside.

Prepare the filling. You will need:

1 cup boiled veal or beef, minced finely
½ cup finely chopped fatback
½ cup breadcrumbs first soaked in milk, then drained well
1 onion, chopped

2 eggs
1 tablespoon fennel seeds or chopped
   dill
Salt and pepper
Egg yolk

Combine all these ingredients and put a little filling on one corner of each *piroshki*. Fold the other side over to form a triangle and pinch the edges together gently. Brush the surface with egg yolk and put them on a greased baking sheet. Bake in a preheated 400° oven until golden brown, about 15 minutes.

27
MEAT PIROSHKI, No. 2

Prepare the dough as in the master recipe above. For this filling you will need:

1 large onion, chopped
1 tablespoon butter
1½ cups boiled beef, veal, or chicken,
   ground
6 sardines, minced

Sauté the onion in the butter, then mix in the meat and the sardines off the heat. Continue as in the master recipe.

You can make another version of this filling using anchovies instead of sardines, along with bread-crumbs soaked in a little milk and drained, and an egg.

You can also make the *piroshki* in the shape of half-moons or even

Meat Piroshki, No. 1

165

rectangles, putting one square over the other. Or roll the rectangles of dough around tin tubes and fry them like that, forming hollow rolls, which can then be stuffed. Of course since they are not cooked again, they should be stuffed with a filling that does not require further cooking.

28
PIROSHKI WITH BRAINS FILLING

For 6 servings, you will need:

Basic *piroshki* dough, prepared as in recipe 26
8–10 ounces calf brains
3 tablespoons vinegar
Peppercorns
Bay leaf
Salt
1 tablespoon butter
1 large onion, chopped
2 tablespoons flour
2 tablespoons cream
Nutmeg
¼ cup parsley, chopped
1 tablespoon lemon juice

Blanch the brains in water to cover with the vinegar, peppercorns, salt and bay leaf for 20 minutes. Drain well and cool. Clean them and cut into pieces. Make a *soffritto* by sautéing the onion in the butter, then add the flour and mix well to bind them. Add the cream and stir well, letting it come to a boil. At this point add

Piroshki with Brains Filling

the brains, then, one at a time, a dash of nutmeg, the parsley, salt, and just at the last minute, the lemon juice. This should cook long enough to make a thick sauce. Continue as in recipe 26. This recipe also works well with *piroshki* shaped in tubes, which should be filled while the dough is still warm.

29
PIROSHSKI WITH LIVER FILLING, No. 1

For 6 servings, you will need:

Basic *piroshki* dough, recipe 26
2½ cups chopped liver, cooked
2 tablespoons butter
1 large onion, chopped
2 eggs
Salt and pepper

Brown the onion in the butter then put it in a bowl. Add the liver, the eggs, onion, salt and pepper and fill the *piroshki* as in recipe 26.

30
PIROSHKI WITH LIVER FILLING, No. 2

For 6 servings you will need:

Basic *piroshki* dough, prepared as in recipe 26, in hollow tubes or triangles
1¼ pounds liver
½ cup chopped fatback
1 onion, chopped
Pepper
2 bay leaves

1 tablespoon oil

1 tablespoon butter

½ cup breadcrumbs, soaked in milk and squeezed dry

3 tablespoons Madeira or Marsala

1 tablespoon rum

Salt

Nutmeg

Clean the liver and cut it into thin slices. Make a *soffritto* by sautéing the onion in the fatback, then add the liver, a little pepper, and the bay leaves. Cook very briefly so the liver doesn't get tough. Remove it from the heat, remove the bay leaves, and pound it in a mortar, adding, little by little, the oil, the butter, the breadcrumbs, Madeira or Marsala, rum, and a pinch of nutmeg and salt. This can also be done in a blender, though the texture is slightly different. Use this mixture to stuff the tubes or triangles and continue as in recipe 26.

31
PIROSHKI WITH FISH FILLING

For six people you will need:

Basic *piroshki* dough, prepared as in recipe 26

3 tablespooons butter

1 medium onion, chopped

1 pound pike or other freshwater fish, poached

1 or 2 hard-boiled eggs, cut in cubes

Salt and pepper

Piroshki with Liver Filling, No. 2 (left)
Piroshki with Shrimp Filling (right)

Make a *soffritto* by sautéing the onion in the butter, then add the fish, the eggs, salt and pepper. Let this mixture cook for a minute to blend, then use it to stuff the *piroshki*.

32
PIROSHKI WITH SHRIMP FILLING

For 6 servings, you will need:

Basic *piroshki* dough, prepared as in recipe 26

24 medium shrimp, boiled, cleaned, and cut up into very small pieces (keep the shells)

4 tablespoons butter

1 tablespoon flour

2 tablespoons cream

Nutmeg

Salt and pepper

3 egg yolks

Pound or grind the shrimp shells into a paste, then let them cook in the butter a few minutes and pass through a fine sieve. Let this cool, making a shrimp butter. Heat this shrimp butter in a pan, add the shrimp meat, the flour, the cream, a pinch of nutmeg, salt and pepper, stirring constantly. Remove from the heat when the cream has thickened, and add the egg yolks. Put this back over a very low heat,

169

stirring and watching it carefully so the eggs do not curdle. As soon as it thickens, remove it and fill the *piroshki* as in recipe 26.

33
PIROSHKI WITH MUSHROOM FILLING

For 6 servings you will need:

Basic *piroshki* dough, prepared as in recipe 26
4 tablespoons butter
1 large onion, chopped
1 cup chopped mushrooms
1 tablespoon flour
3 tablespoons cream
2 hard-boiled eggs, diced
Salt and pepper

Sauté the onion in the butter, then add the mushrooms. Sprinkle the flour over them to thicken and cook this a few minutes before adding the cream, eggs, salt and pepper. This filling is best for *piroshki* made in the shape of tubes.

34
PIROSHKI WITH CABBAGE FILLING

For 6 servings, you will need:

Basic *piroshki* dough, prepared as in recipe 26
4 tablespoons butter
1 large onion, chopped
1 small cabbage, cut into strips
3 hard-boiled eggs, diced
Salt and pepper

Focaccine, Peking Style

Make a *soffritto* by sautéing the chopped onion in the butter, then add the cabbage and cook over moderate heat until the cabbage is thoroughly cooked. Remove from the heat and add the eggs, salt, and pepper. Blend this well and fill *piroshki* shaped like tubes.

35
FOCACCINE, PEKING STYLE

These are *focaccine* meant to go with various foods, as a bread substitute. For 6 servings you will need:

4 cups flour
Salt
Hot water
Oil

Work together the flour, a pinch of salt, and enough hot water, added little by little, to make a very firm but pliable dough. Roll it out into a rectangle ¾ inch thick and cut it into 2¼-inch squares. Brush half of them generously with oil, and cover with the others. Fry them in pairs in a hot oiled skillet.

They can be served, while still hot, with pieces of roasted or boiled meat, an omelet cut into strips, fried bean sprouts moistened with soy sauce, strips of cabbage, browned in a pan and flavored with soy sauce, and so on.

36
QUICHE LORRAINE

This celebrated dish is similar to a cheese *crostata*. For 6 servings, you will need:

1⅔ cups flour
⅔ cups butter or lard, softened
Salt
Handful dried beans

Work the flour together with the butter and add a pinch of salt and enough water to get a soft but firm dough. Roll out a circle about ¼ inch thick and line a lightly greased baking pan or pie pan with it, so that it extends up the sides a little. Prick it with a fork, spread the beans on the bottom to weight

Quiche Lorraine

it, and partially cook it in a preheated oven at 350°, until the pastry is set but not browned. Remove the beans. For the filling you will need:

1½ cups chopped smoked bacon or ham
1½ cups cubed or grated Swiss or Gruyère cheese
3 eggs
1 cup cream
Salt and pepper
Butter

Spread the bacon or ham and cheese over the dough. Beat the eggs and add the cream, salt and pepper to them and pour over the

171

bacon. Put small bits of butter over the top and bake in a preheated 350° oven until the eggs have set and the crust is golden.

37
MEAT KULIBIAKI

From the grand cuisine of Russia, this is a kind of *torta rustica* filled with meat and other ingredients. For 6 servings you will need:

3¼ cups flour
Salt
2 eggs
¾ cup butter, softened

Add a dash of salt to the flour and work it together with the eggs and butter, adding just enough water to make a very soft but well-blended dough. Shape it into a ball and let it rest in a cool place, under a cloth. Meanwhile, prepare the filling. You will need:

2 cups cooked minced meat (leftovers are fine)
2–3 onions, chopped and cooked
1½ cups chopped mushrooms, sautéed briefly in oil
Salt and pepper
3 hard-boiled eggs, in wedges
Beaten egg yolk

Blend well the meat, onions, mushrooms, salt and pepper to taste. Roll the dough out into a ¼-inch-thick rectangle and spread the filling over the dough, leaving a border of about ½ inch. On top of

Fish Kulibiaki

the filling place the wedges of hard-boiled eggs, pushing them into the filling a little. Finally roll the dough up over the filling, forming a kind of rustic strudel. Pinch the ends and seam together so that the edges stick and paint the surface with beaten egg yolk. Place it seam side down on a well-greased baking pan and put in a preheated 375° oven for 25 minutes or until the dough has turned golden brown.

38
FISH KULIBIAKI

This recipe is almost the same as the one above except that you use fish instead of meat. The onions and hard-boiled eggs are usually eliminated. Instead you can add parsley and grated lemon peel.

39
CHEESE KULIBIAKI

This *kulibiaki* is made with 1½ cups of a fresh cheese like Ricotta, to which you can add eggs, mushrooms, onions, and other vegetables in combinations to satisfy almost any taste. Roll and bake as in recipe 37.

40
MUSHROOM KULIBIAKI

This is almost the same as the cheese *kulibiaki* except that the

main ingredient is 2 cups of chopped mushrooms; the cheese is reduced to ½ cup or less. You can also add peeled, seeded and cubed tomatoes. Two raw beaten eggs can also be incorporated into the filling, but then of course you should eliminate the hard-boiled ones.

173